UNIT 15 (30)

Transition Elements

First published 1984
by John Murray (Publishers) Ltd
50 Albemarle Street
London W1X 4BD

Printed and bound in Great Britain by
Martin's of Berwick

British Library Cataloguing in Publication Data

Independent Learning Project for Advanced
Chemistry
Transition Elements. - (ILPAC; Unit I5)
1. Science
I. Title II. Series
500 Q161.2

ISBN 0 7195 4053 4

CONTENTS

PREFACE

This volume is one of twenty Units produced by ILPAC, the Independent Learning Project for Advanced Chemistry, written for students preparing for the Advanced Level examinations of the G.C.E. The Project has been sponsored by the Inner London Education Authority and the materials have been extensively tested in London schools and colleges. In its present revised form, however, it is intended for a wider audience; the syllabuses of all the major Examination Boards have been taken into account and questions set by these boards have been included.

Although ILPAC was initially conceived as a way of overcoming some of the difficulties presented by uneconomically small sixth forms, it has frequently been adopted because its approach to learning has certain advantages over more traditional teaching methods. Students assume a greater responsibility for their own learning and can work, to some extent, at their own pace, while teachers can devote more time to guiding individual students and to managing resources.

By providing personal guidance, and detailed solutions to the many exercises, supported by the optional use of video-cassettes, the Project allows students to study A-level chemistry with less teacher-contact time than a conventional course demands. The extent to which this is possible must be determined locally; potentially hazardous practical work must, of course, be supervised. Nevertheless, flexibility in time-tabling makes ILPAC an attractive proposition in situations where classes are small or suitably-qualified teachers are scarce.

In addition, ILPAC can provide at least a partial solution to other problems. Students with only limited access to laboratories, for example, those studying at evening classes, can concentrate upon ILPAC practical work in the laboratory, in the confidence that related theory can be systematically studied elsewhere. Teachers of A-level chemistry who are inexperienced, or whose main discipline is another science, will find ILPAC very supportive. The materials can be used effectively where upper and lower sixth form classes are timetabled together. ILPAC can provide 'remedial' material for students in higher education. Schools operating sixth form consortia can benefit from the cohesion that ILPAC can provide in a fragmented situation. The project can be adapted for use in parts of the world where there is a severe shortage of qualified chemistry teachers. And so on.

A more detailed introduction to ILPAC, with specific advice both to students and to teachers, is included in the first volume only. Details of the Project Team and Trial Schools appear inside the back cover.

LONDON 1983

ACKNOWLEDGEMENTS

Thanks are due to the following examination boards for permission to reproduce questions from past A-level papers:

Joint Matriculation Board;

Teacher-marked Exercise, p62(3)(1980)

Oxford Delegacy of Local Examinations;

Teacher-marked Exercise, p77(1981)

Southern Universities Joint Board;

End-of-Unit Test 13(1982)

The Associated Examining Board;

Exercise 10(1980)
Teacher-marked Exercise p78(1980)
Level One Test 11(1980)

University of London Entrance and School Examinations Council;

Exercises 27(1981), 51(N1978)
Teacher-marked Exercises p25(1977), p62(1)(1974), p62(2)(N1982)
Level One Test 1-5(1983), 6(1977), 7(1978), 8(1977), 9(1981)
10(1979), 12(1983)
End-of-Unit Test 1-4(1978), 5(N1975), 6(1979), 7(N1978), 8(N1980)
9(1980), 10(1981), 11(1977), 12(1980), 14(1976)
15(1976), 16a(1981), 16b(1982)

Where answers to these questions are included, they are provided by ILPAC and not by the examination boards.

Questions from papers of other examining boards appear in other Units.

Photographs are reproduced by permission as follows:

Fig. 6: Space shuttle - Popperfoto
Fig. 7A: Brass - J. Allan Cash Photolibrary
Fig. 7B, 7C, 7D, 7F - Tony Langham
Fig. 7E: Railway lines - Popperfoto
Fig. 9: Blast furnace - Popperfoto
Fig. 10: Steel production - Popperfoto
Fig. 11: Atomic models - Tony Langham
Photographs of students - Tony Langham

SYMBOLS USED IN ILPAC UNITS

Reading

Exercise

Test

'A' Level question

'A' Level part question

'A' Level question Special paper

Worked example

Teacher-marked exercise

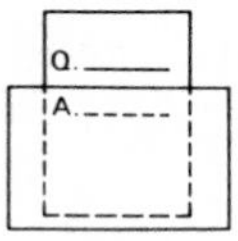
Revealing exercises

Discussion

Computer programme

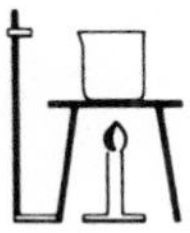
Experiment

Video programme

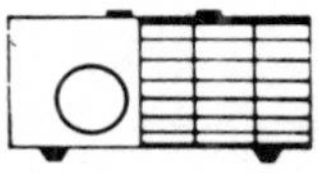
Film loop

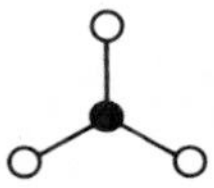
Model-making

INTERNATIONAL HAZARD SYMBOLS

Harmful

Toxic

Radioactive

Flammable

Explosive

Corrosive

Oxidising

INTRODUCTION

The term 'transition elements' can include all the elements in the central part of the Periodic Table - between the block of typical metals in Groups I and II and the block of elements, mostly non-metals, in Groups III to 0. This position helps to explain the use of the word 'transition', although the term is not altogether satisfactory. You have probably already used the term '*d*-block' instead in your study of the Periodic Table as a whole, although this too is not entirely satisfactory.

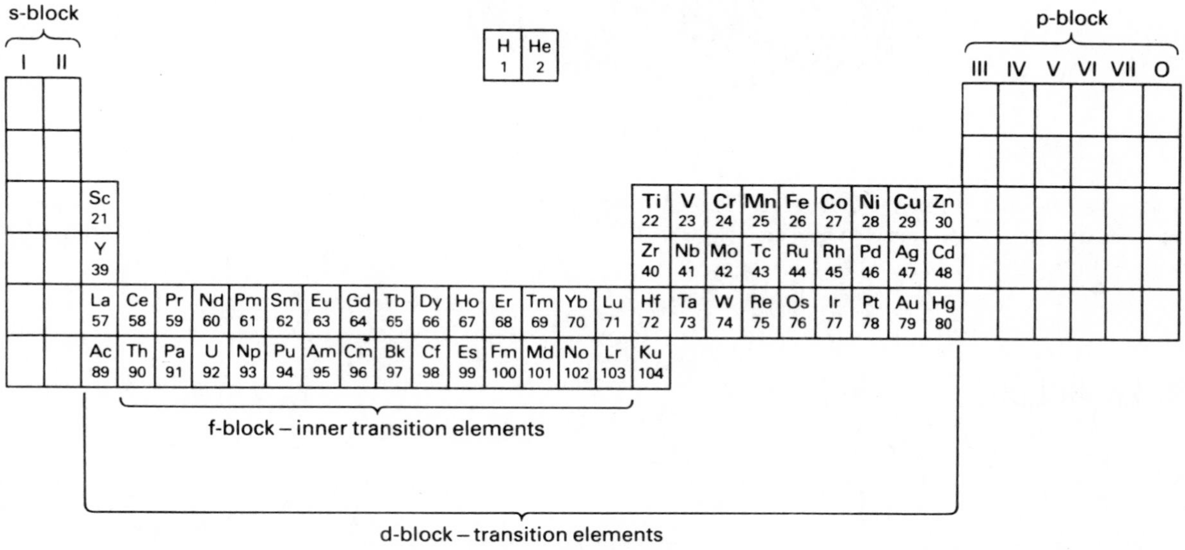

Fig.1. The Periodic Table

We confine a detailed study in this Unit to the elements $_{21}Sc$ to $_{30}Zn$, although the discussion is sometimes limited to the elements $_{22}Ti$ to $_{29}Cu$ for reasons which we explain. Many of the general statements apply also to the other rows. The whole block is characterised by similarity of properties, not only in vertical groups as elsewhere in the Periodic Table, but in horizontal rows as well.

In Level One of this Unit we explore the general properties which are characteristic of transition elements, especially variable oxidation states. We use standard electrode potentials, $E^{\ominus}$, to determine the feasibility of reaction, as described in Unit P6 (Equilibrium III: Redox Reactions). At the end of Level One we include a Section on the extraction of iron from its ores in the blast furnace. If you need to study Ellingham diagrams in this connection you should look at Appendix One at this point.

We extend your study of the general characteristics of transition elements in Level Two, where we consider more fully the formation and stability of complex ions and the mechanism of homogeneous catalysis. In Appendix Two you can, if you wish, take your study of complex ions a little beyond A-level in order to consider a more satisfactory explanation of variations in colour and paramagnetism.

There is a video-programme entitled 'Transition Metals' made to accompany this Unit. It is not essential but, if it is available, you should try to see it at the appropriate times. You might watch it right through before you start the Unit, and later use sections to help you with individual topics.

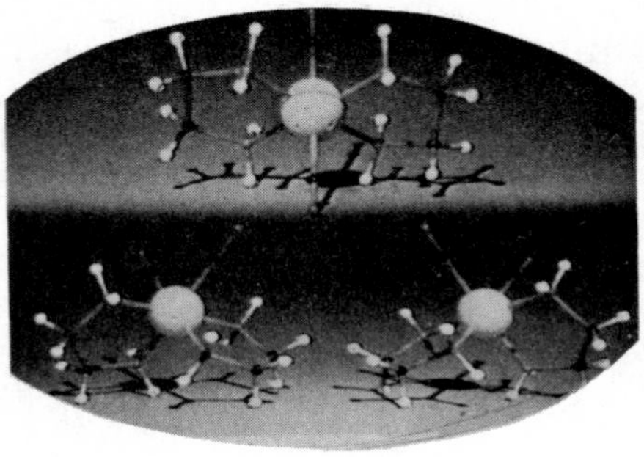

Transition metals

There are seven experiments in this Unit, two in Level One and five in Level Two. Your teacher may advise you not to do all of them. There is also an end-of-Unit practical test.

PRE-KNOWLEDGE

Before you start work on this Unit, you should be able to:

(1) identify the *d*-block in an outline Periodic Table;

(2) write electron configurations for elements up to $_{22}$Sc both in *s, p, d* notation and in 'electrons in boxes' form;

(3) deduce oxidation numbers of elements in compounds, given their formulae;

(4) use standard electrode potentials to predict the feasibility of redox reactions;

(5) recognise examples of different types of isomerism;

(6) write an expression for the equilibrium constant for a given reaction.

PRE-TEST

To find out whether you are ready to start Level One, try the following test. You should not spend more than 40 minutes on this test. Hand your answers to your teacher for marking.

PRE-TEST

1. Write electron configurations in *s*, *p*, *d* notation for the element ${}_{13}Al$ and the ion ${}_{8}O^{2-}$. (2)

2. Write electron configurations in 'electrons in boxes' form for the element N and the ion K^+. (2)

3. Use the simple rules to calculate the oxidation number of phosphorus in these compounds and ions:

   (a) PH_4^+ (b) H_3PO_4 (c) $H_2PO_3^-$ (d) P_4O_6 (4)

4. Use the following electrode potentials to write balanced equations, with appropriate $\Delta E^\ominus$ values, for

   (a) a reaction which probably goes to completion,

   (b) a reaction for which the equilibrium mixture contains a significant proportion of both reactants and products.

   $Zn^{2+}(aq) + 2e^- \rightleftharpoons Zn(s)$ $E^\ominus = -0.76$ V

   $Cr^{3+}(aq) + 3e^- \rightleftharpoons Cr(s)$ $E^\ominus = -0.74$ V

   $Ag^+(aq) + e^- \rightleftharpoons Ag(s)$ $E^\ominus = +0.80$ V (4)

   Why was the word 'probably' used above? (1)

5. Write an expression for the equilibrium constant for the reaction:

   $Cu^{2+}(aq) + 4NH_3(aq) \rightleftharpoons Cu(NH_3)_4^{2+}(aq)$ (2)

   What is the unit for this constant? (1)

6. Select from the following structures, all of which are trichlorobut-1-enes:

   (a) two geometric isomers,

   (b) two optical isomers,

   (c) two structural isomers.

   Name the isomers in each pair, showing how prefixes are used to distinguish between the two. (In (b) you are not expected to know which is which!)

(i)

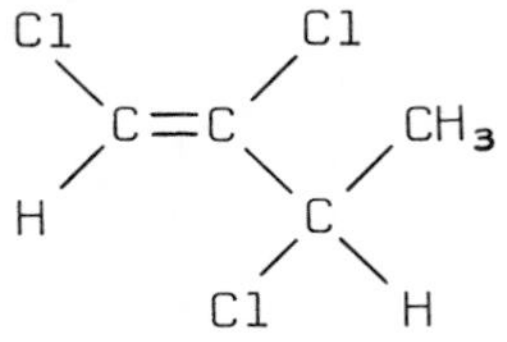

(iii)

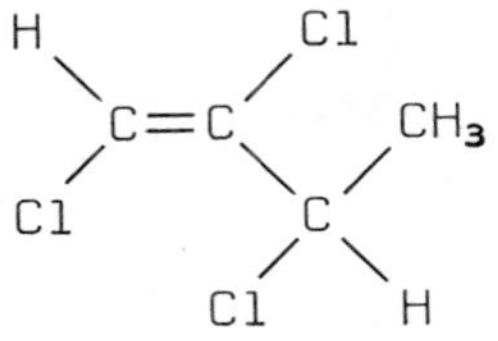

(ii)

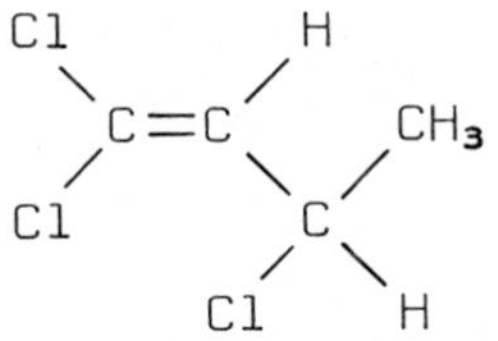

(iv)

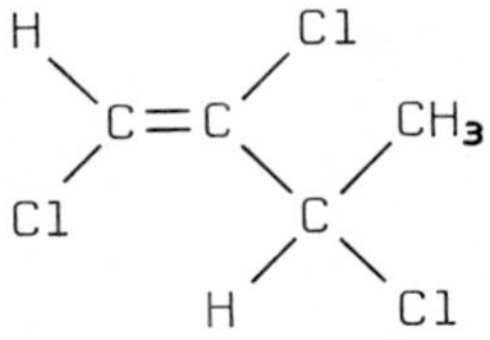

(9)

(Total 25 marks)

LEVEL ONE

The metals you have studied so far, those in Groups I and II, each have a single oxidation state. In the transition elements you study metals which each have several oxidation states, and this is the key to much of their characteristic chemistry.

VARIABLE OXIDATION STATE

Objectives. When you have finished this section you should be able to:

(1) write electron configurations for the atoms of the first transition series from scandium to zinc;

(2) write electron configurations for some of the more common ions of transition elements;

(3) explain why transition elements have variable oxidation states;

(4) explain the general pattern of oxidation states in the transition elements;

(5) explain why scandium and zinc are often excluded from the study of transition elements.

Electron configurations of the elements

First, read the introductory section of the chapter on transition elements in your textbook(s). For the time being, focus your attention on electron configurations and oxidation states. Other characteristics, such as catalysis, complex ions, colour and paramagnetism will be mentioned, but you will study these more fully later in the Unit.

Exercise 1 (a) Write down the electron configurations, in *s*, *p*, *d* notation, for the elements $_{21}Sc$ to $_{30}Zn$. Show all the sub-shells for scandium but thereafter represent the electron arrangement which is common to all by the symbol of a noble gas.

(b) Write down the electron configurations again, but this time use the 'electrons-in-boxes' notation for the $3d$ and $4s$ orbitals.

(Answers on page 81)

You have noted that atoms of chromium and copper have only one $4s$ electron, whereas all the others have two. For the next exercise, find out from your textbook(s) why this is so. You may find it useful to revise from Unit S2 (Atomic Structure) an explanation of the 'steps' between nitrogen and oxygen and between phosphorus and sulphur in the plots of ionization energy against atomic number.

Exercise 2 (a) Suggest reasons why atoms of chromium and copper have only one $4s$ electron while the other elements in the full transition series have two $4s$ electrons.

(b) What would you expect to be the electron configurations of molybdenum and silver atoms?

(Answers on page 81)

Having considered the electronic structure of atoms, we now consider the loss of electrons to form ions.

Formation of ions

The first point to grasp is that when transition elements form ions it is always the s-electrons which are lost first. You have learned that in the hypothetical process of 'building up' atoms by adding electrons and protons one by one the $4s$ orbitals are filled before the $3d$ - you might therefore expect the $3d$ electrons to be lost first.

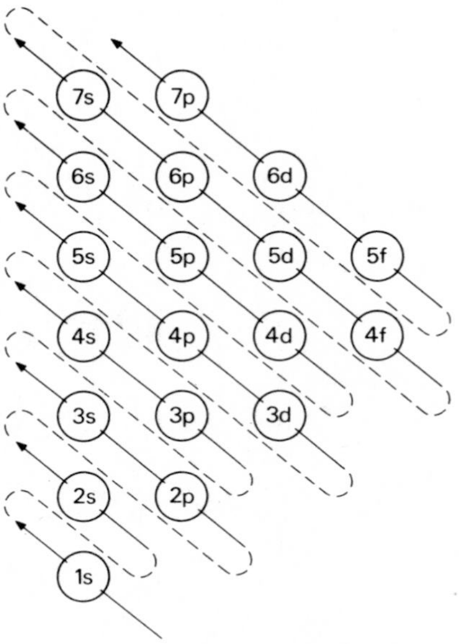

Fig.2. The order in which orbitals are filled.

$3d$ electrons would be lost first if protons were lost at the same time but, of course, in the formation of ions, only electrons are lost, leaving the atom with an excess positive charge. This excess charge has the effect of pulling all the electrons a little closer and, in the process, the $3d$ orbitals occupy a lower energy level than the $4s$.

This is one consequence of the fact that the $3d$ and $4s$ energy levels are fairly close together for the transition elements, as shown in Fig. 3. At scandium, the effect is that the energy levels are 'inverted' and the energy of the $3d$ orbitals is less than that of the $4s$.

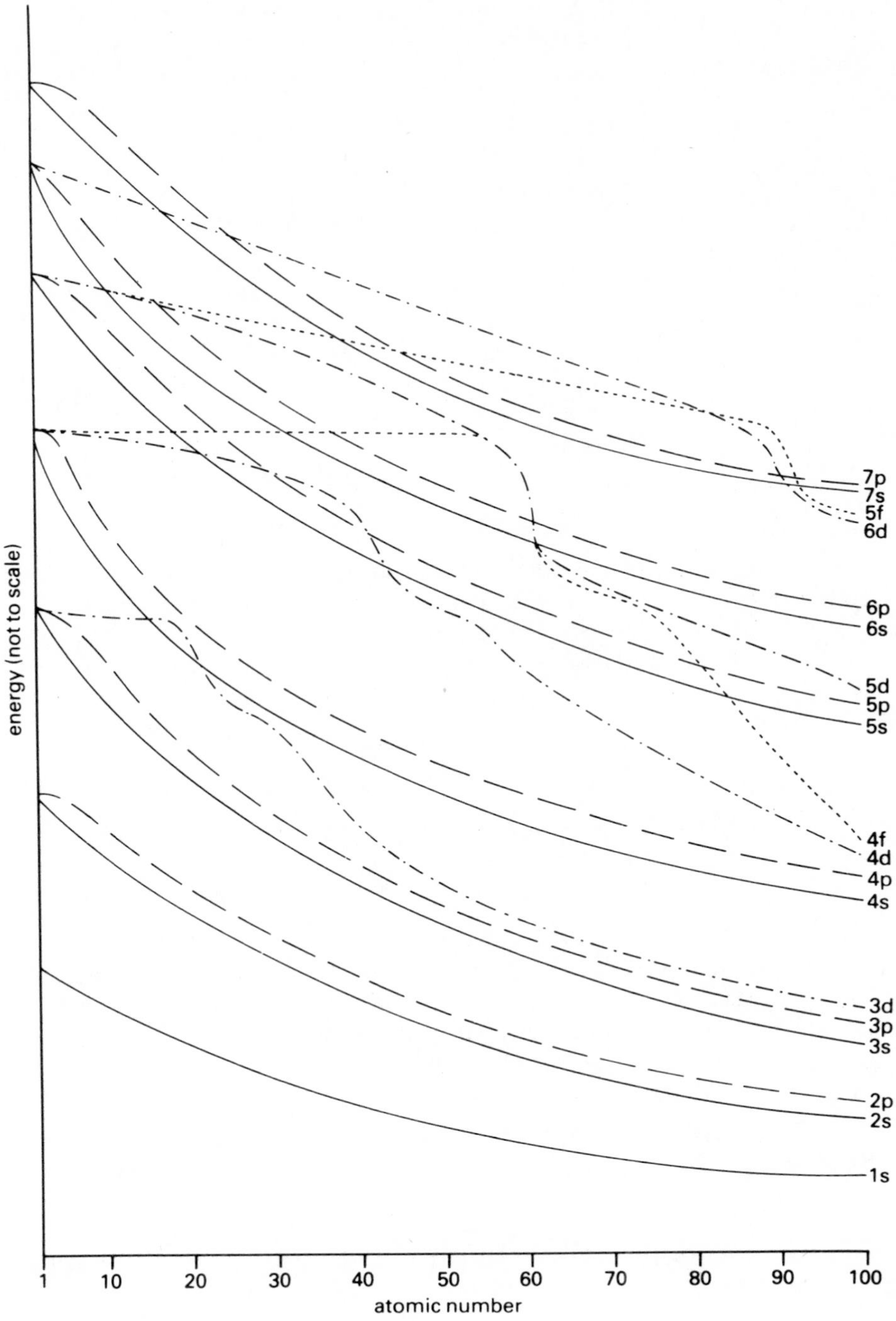

Fig.3. Variation of energy levels with atomic number.

You should now be able to see that a number of different electron configurations could be reasonably stable for ions of transition elements, instead of the more usual single stable configuration for other metals.

Draw together what you have learned about stable electron configurations, in this Unit and earlier, in order to do the next exercise.

<u>Exercise 3</u> Consider the loss of electrons one at a time from typical transition elements. What resulting electron configurations do you think might be reasonably stable?

(Answer on page 81)

Most transition elements do indeed form a number of different ions, and their configurations often conform to the criteria for stability we listed in our answer to Exercise 3. However, other configurations are stable, as you see in the next exercise.

Exercise 4 Write 'electrons-in-boxes' configurations for the following ions, all of which exist although some are more stable than others.

(a) Sc^{3+}	(e) V^{3+}	(i) Fe^{2+}	(m) Ni^{2+}
(b) Ti^{2+}	(f) Cr^{+}	(j) Fe^{3+}	(n) Cu^{+}
(c) Ti^{3+}	(g) Cr^{3+}	(k) Co^{2+}	(o) Cu^{2+}
(d) V^{2+}	(h) Mn^{2+}	(l) Co^{3+}	(p) Zn^{2+}

(Answers on page 81)

The stability of a particular ion depends to some extent on the anion with which it combines. For instance, fluoride, and to a lesser extent chloride, which are small and not easily polarized, stabilize high oxidation states. On the other hand, iodide, and to a lesser extent bromide, stabilize lower oxidation states.

The pattern of oxidation states

Ions with charges greater than 3+ are rarely found, but higher oxidation states than 3 or 4 (in which the electrons may be regarded as 'partially lost' to more electronegative atoms in covalent bonding) are very common in compounds of the transition elements. Remember that, in this context, oxidation number is merely a formalism and does not relate to the actual charge on the atom in the compound.

Higher oxidation states are most often seen in oxides and oxo-anions, some of which are the subject of the next exercise.

Exercise 5 Work out the oxidation states of the transition elements in the following ions and compounds:

(a) MnO_4^-	(e) K_2CrO_4	(i) $VOCl_2$
(b) MnO_2	(f) Cr_2O_3	(j) V_2O_5
(c) K_2MnO_4	(g) $KCrO_3Cl$	(k) NH_4VO_3
(d) $Cr_2O_7^{2-}$	(h) VO_2^+	

(Answers on page 81)

The following table summarises the known oxidation states of elements of the first transition series - the most common states are ringed. Use it to answer the next exercise.

Table 1

Sc	Ti	V	Cr	Mn	Fe	Co	Ni	Cu	Zn
				⑦					
			⑥	6	6				
		⑤	5	5	5	5			
	④	4	4	4	4	4	4		
③	3	3	③	3	③	3	3	3	
	2	2	2	②	②	②	②	②	②
	1	1	1	1	1	1	1	1	

Exercise 6 What patterns can you see in the common oxidation states:

(a) from scandium to manganese,

(b) from manganese to zinc?

(Answers on page 81)

Table 1 shows that scandium and zinc have only one known oxidation state. This sometimes leads to their exclusion from a list of transition metals.

Why scandium and zinc are not typical transition metals

All zinc compounds have a filled $3d$ sub-shell while all scandium compounds have an empty $3d$ sub-shell. The typical properties of compounds of transition elements are associated, as you will see, with partly-filled d orbitals. For this reason, scandium and zinc may be excluded from a study of transition elements. We will mention another reason for their exclusion when we deal with physical properties.

In the next section you study experimentally some of the oxidation states of two typical transition elements, vanadium and manganese.

REDOX CHEMISTRY OF VANADIUM AND MANGANESE

Objectives. When you have finished this section you should be able to:

(6) describe the preparation of a variety of oxidation states for vanadium and manganese;

(7) describe some examples of disproportionation and reverse disproportionation involving vanadium and manganese.

Vanadium

The oxidation states of vanadium are best illustrated by an experiment which you can see in the section of the ILPAC video-programme 'Transition Metals' dealing with variable oxidation states.

However, you should, if possible, do the experiment yourself.

EXPERIMENT 1

Illustrating the oxidation states of vanadium

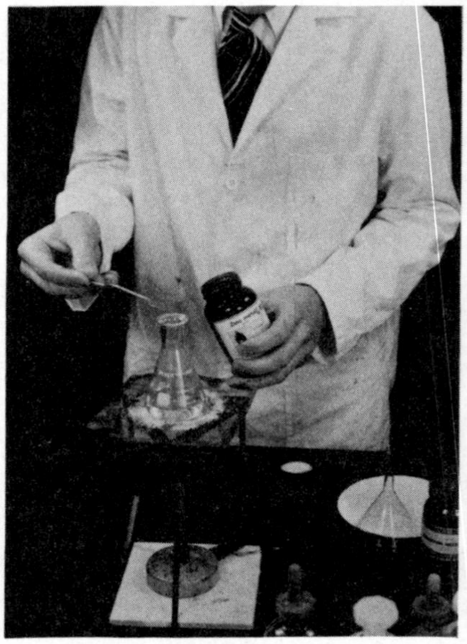

Aim

The purpose of this experiment is to illustrate the presence of several different oxidation states for vanadium, and to show how it is possible to change from one oxidation state to another.

Introduction

Starting with a solution containing vanadium(V) in acid conditions, you use powdered zinc as a reducing agent. Colour changes indicate the formation of other oxidation states. After this first series of reactions you perform some changes between oxidation states by using a variety of oxidizing and reducing agents.

Requirements

safety spectacles and gloves
conical flask, 100 cm^3
spatula
ammonium polytrioxovanadate(V), NH_4VO_3 (ammonium metavanadate)
measuring cylinder, 25 cm^3
sulphuric acid, dilute, 1 M H_2SO_4
sulphuric acid, concentrated, H_2SO_4
5 test-tubes and holder
test-tube rack
zinc dust, Zn
Bunsen burner, tripod, gauze and bench mat
filter funnel and paper
potassium manganate(VII) solution, 0.02 M $KMnO_4$ (permanganate)
sodium sulphite, Na_2SO_3
potassium iodide solution, 0.05 M KI
sodium thiosulphate solution, 0.1 M $Na_2S_2O_3$

Hazard warning

Concentrated sulphuric acid is corrosive and reacts violently with water. Therefore you MUST

WEAR SAFETY SPECTACLES AND GLOVES.
WHEN DILUTING, ADD ACID TO WATER, NOT WATER TO ACID.
MOP UP SMALL SPILLAGES WITH EXCESS WATER.

Procedure

First complete a copy of Table 2 to assist you in identifying the different oxidation states of vanadium.

Table 2

Ion (hydrated)	$^*VO_2{}^+$	VO^{2+}	V^{3+}	V^{2+}
Colour	yellow	blue	green	violet
Oxidation state				
Name				

(Answer on page 82)

*The $VO_3{}^-$ ion in the ammonium salt is converted to $VO_2{}^+$ by acid:

$$VO_3{}^-(aq) + 2H^+(aq) \rightleftharpoons VO_2{}^+(aq) + H_2O(l)$$

1. Place about 0.25 g (one spatula measure) of ammonium trioxovanadate(V) in a conical flask and add about 25 cm^3 of dilute sulphuric acid. Carefully add about 5 cm^3 of concentrated sulphuric acid and swirl the flask until you obtain a clear yellow solution.
2. Pour about 2 cm^3 of this vanadium(V) solution into each of two test-tubes ready for later tests.
3. To the conical flask add 1 - 2 g (one spatula measure) of zinc dust, a little at a time. Swirl the flask at intervals and record any observed colour changes in a copy of Results Table 1.
4. When the solution has become violet (you may need to heat the flask for this final change), filter about 2 cm^3 into each of three test-tubes.
5. To one of the three tubes add, a little at a time, an excess of acidified potassium manganate(VII) solution, shaking after each addition, until no further change is observed.
6. Keep the other test-tubes of solutions for later tests. Answer the first two questions (page 12) and complete Results Table 1 as far as you can before doing further tests.
7. To one of the tubes containing vanadium(V) add a little sodium sulphite and shake. Filter if cloudy. Now boil carefully (at a fume cupboard) to remove excess sulphur dioxide and add about the same volume of the vanadium(II) solution. Record your observations.
8. To the second of the tubes containing vanadium(V), add about 2 cm^3 potassium iodide solution and mix. Then add about 2 cm^3 of sodium thiosulphate solution. Record your observations.
9. Keep the last tube of vanadium(II) solution for a final experiment you may wish to do after answering question 7.

Results Table 1

Test	Observations	Summary of reaction
Ammonium vanadate + acid	White solid dissolved to a yellow solution.	$\overset{+5}{VO_3^-} \rightarrow \overset{+5}{VO_2^+}$
Vanadium(V) + zinc		
Vanadium(II) + manganate(VII)		
Vanadium(V) + sulphite Add vanadium(II)		
Vanadium(V) + iodide + thiosulphate		
Vanadium(II) + - - - - -		

(Specimen results on page 82)

Questions

1. How do you explain the first appearance of a green colour in the solution?

2. What are the subsequent changes in colour and why do these changes occur?

You will need the following electrode potentials in order to answer some of the remaining questions:

$Zn^{2+}(aq) + 2e^- \rightleftharpoons Zn(s)$ $E^\ominus = -0.76$ V

$V^{3+}(aq) + e^- \rightleftharpoons V^{2+}(aq)$ $E^\ominus = -0.26$ V

$VO^{2+}(aq) + 2H^+(aq) + e^- \rightleftharpoons V^{3+}(aq) + H_2O(l)$ $E^\ominus = +0.34$ V

$VO_2^+(aq) + 2H^+(aq) + e^- \rightleftharpoons VO^{2+}(aq) + H_2O(l)$ $E^\ominus = +1.00$ V

$SO_4^{2-}(aq) + 4H^+(aq) + 2e^- \rightleftharpoons H_2SO_3(aq) + H_2O(l)$ $E^\ominus = +0.17$ V

$I_2(aq) + 2e^- \rightleftharpoons 2I^-(aq)$ $E^\ominus = +0.54$ V

3. What did you observe when you added iodide ions to vanadium(V)? What caused this colour?

4. Why did you add sodium thiosulphate?

5. Why does reduction with iodide not give the same result as reduction with zinc?

6. What did you observe when you added sulphite ions to acidified vanadium(V) solution? Does this result correspond with a prediction made using the $E^\ominus$ values? (Hint: sulphite ions and acid react to give what?)

7. How would you set about finding a suitable oxidizing agent for the oxidation of vanadium(II) to vanadium(III) and no further? Does one appear in the table above?

(Answers on page 82)

In the next section we consider the various oxidation states of manganese.

The oxidation states of manganese

The worked example and exercises which follow help you to predict ways of making the less common oxidation states of manganese from the readily available Mn(VII), Mn(IV) and Mn(II). You may then test your predictions in Experiment 2.

Worked example. It has been proposed that Mn(VI) compounds might be formed by reaction between Mn(VII) and Mn(IV). Predict the feasibility of such reactions in aqueous solution of varying pH.

W

Solution.

The first requirement is to find electrode potentials for appropriate half-cells. These are quoted for 'standard' acid conditions, namely $[H^+(aq)] = 1\ mol\ dm^{-3}$ or pH = 0:

(VII → VI): $2MnO_4^-(aq) + 2e^- \rightleftharpoons 2MnO_4^{2-}(aq)$; $E^\ominus = 0.56$ V

(VI → IV): $MnO_4^{2-}(aq) + 4H^+(aq) + 2e^- \rightleftharpoons MnO_2(s) + 2H_2O(l)$; $E^\ominus = 2.26$ V

A cell reaction converting Mn(VII) and Mn(IV) to Mn(VI) is obtained by reversing the second half-equation and adding to the first:

$2MnO_4^-(aq) + MnO_2(s) + 2H_2O(l) \rightleftharpoons 3MnO_4^{2-}(aq) + 4H^+(aq)$;

$\Delta E^\ominus = -2.26\ V + 0.56\ V = -1.70\ V$

Since $\Delta E^\ominus$ is large and negative, the reaction will not proceed from left to right to any measurable extent. Indeed, any Mn(VI) obtained by other means would be expected to disproportionate completely in acid conditions. (The same conclusion may be reached by applying the 'anticlockwise rule' to the two half-equations.)

We also see that reducing $[H^+(aq)]$ would shift equilibrium to the right and make the desired reaction more likely. We should therefore consider alkaline conditions.

Electrode potentials for 'standard' alkaline conditions, namely $[OH^-(aq)] = 1\ mol\ dm^{-3}$ or pH = 14, are as follows:

(VII → VI): $2MnO_4^-(aq) + 2e^- \rightleftharpoons 2MnO_4^{2-}(aq)$; $E^\ominus = 0.56$ V

(VI → IV): $MnO_4^{2-}(aq) + 2H_2O(l) + 2e^- \rightleftharpoons MnO_2(s) + 4OH^-(aq)$; $E^\ominus = 0.60$ V

A cell reaction converting Mn(VII) and Mn(IV) to Mn(VI) is obtained by reversing the second half-equation and adding to the first:

$2MnO_4^-(aq) + MnO_2(s) + 4OH^-(aq) \rightleftharpoons 3MnO_4^{2-}(aq) + 2H_2O(l)$; $\Delta E^\ominus = -0.04$ V

Here we see that $\Delta E^\ominus$ is negative again, but this time very small, so that we might expect the reaction to produce an equilibrium mixture containing significant proportions of both reactants and products. Furthermore, we should be able to shift the equilibrium to the right by increasing $[OH^-(aq)]$, thus producing more Mn(VI) in the equilibrium mixture.

You can test this prediction in Experiment 2, together with predictions you make in the next three exercises.

Exercise 7 Predict the feasibility of making Mn(III) from Mn(II) and Mn(IV) under conditions of varying pH. Use these electrode potentials:

$MnO_2(s) + 4H^+(aq) + e^- \rightleftharpoons Mn^{3+}(aq) + 2H_2O(l)$; $E^\ominus = 0.95$ V

$Mn^{3+}(aq) + e^- \rightleftharpoons Mn^{2+}(aq)$; $E^\ominus = 1.51$ V

$Mn(OH)_3(s) + e^- \rightleftharpoons Mn(OH)_2(s) + OH^-(aq)$; $E^\ominus = -0.10$ V

$MnO_2(s) + 2H_2O(l) + e^- \rightleftharpoons Mn(OH)_3 + OH^-(aq)$; $E^\ominus = 0.20$ V

(Answer on page **83**)

Exercise 8 Predict the feasibility of making Mn(III) from Mn(II) and Mn(VII) in acid conditions. The relevant half-cell potentials are:

$Mn^{3+}(aq) + e^- \rightleftharpoons Mn^{2+}(aq)$; $E^\ominus = 1.51$ V

$MnO_4^-(aq) + 8H^+(aq) + 5e^- \rightleftharpoons Mn^{2+}(aq) + 4H_2O(l)$; $E^\ominus = 1.50$ V

(Answer on page **83**)

Exercise 9 Predict the feasibility of making Mn(V) from Mn(IV) and Mn(VI) in conditions of varying pH. The relevant half-cell potentials are:

$MnO_4^{2-}(aq) + 2H^+(aq) + e^- \rightleftharpoons MnO_3^-(aq) + H_2O(l)$; $E^\ominus = 2.0$ V

$MnO_3^-(aq) + 2H^+(aq) + e^- \rightleftharpoons MnO_2(s) + H_2O(l)$; $E^\ominus = 2.0$ V

$MnO_4^{2-}(aq) + H_2O(l) + e^- \rightleftharpoons MnO_3^-(aq) + 2OH^-(aq)$; $E^\ominus = 0.34$ V

$MnO_3^-(aq) + H_2O(l) + e^- \rightleftharpoons MnO_2(s) + 2OH^-(aq)$; $E^\ominus = 0.84$ V

(Answer on page **83**)

Now you should be able to do Experiment 2. Be sure to have your answers to the last three exercises available for comparison.

EXPERIMENT 2

The oxidation states of manganese

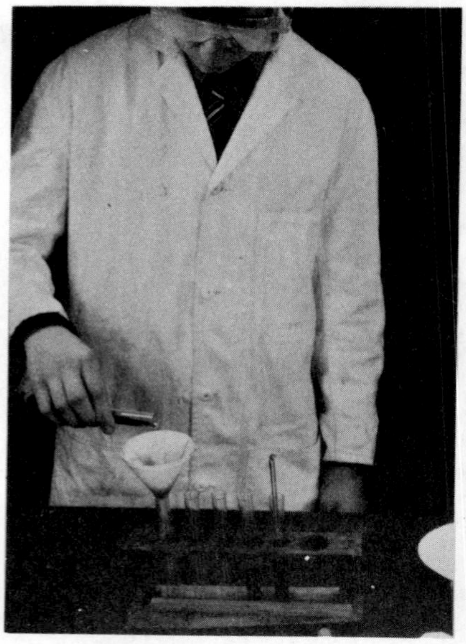

Aim and Introduction

The purpose of this experiment is to make samples of some of the less common oxidation states of manganese, using methods predicted in the previous exercises. There are three parts, with questions following each.

Requirements

safety spectacles and protective gloves
6 test-tubes and rack
potassium manganate(VII) (permanganate) solution, 0.01 M $KMnO_4$
sulphuric acid, dilute, 1 M H_2SO_4
sodium hydroxide solution, 2 M NaOH
manganese(IV) oxide (manganese dioxide), MnO_2
spatula
stirring rod
filter funnel and 3 papers
manganese(II) sulphate-4-water, $MnSO_4 \cdot 4H_2O$
sulphuric acid, concentrated, H_2SO_4

> **Hazard warning**
>
> Concentrated sulphuric acid is corrosive and reacts violently with water. Therefore you MUST:
>
> WEAR SAFETY SPECTACLES AND GLOVES.
> WHEN DILUTING, ADD ACID TO WATER, NOT WATER TO ACID.
> MOP UP SMALL SPILLAGES WITH EXCESS WATER.

Procedure. Part A

Refer to the Worked Example on page 13 where we predicted that it should be possible to make Mn(VI) from Mn(VII) and Mn(IV).

1. Put about 5 cm^3 of potassium manganate(VII) solution in each of three test-tubes.
2. To one of the three tubes add about 3 cm^3 dilute sulphuric acid and to another add about 3 cm^3 sodium hydroxide solution.
3. To each of the three tubes add a little solid manganese(IV) oxide and stir for about a minute.
4. Filter enough of each mixture into a clean tube to see the colour of the filtrate clearly. Use a fresh filter paper for each mixture.
5. One of the tubes should now have in it a clear green solution of Mn(VI). Add to this a little dilute sulphuric acid.

Questions. Part A.

1. Explain why only one of the three mixtures reacted to give green Mn(VI).
2. What happened when acid was added to Mn(VI)? Explain.

(Answers on page 83)

Procedure. Part B

Refer to your answer to Exercise 7 in which you predicted that it should be possible to make Mn(III) from Mn(II) and Mn(VII).

6. Dissolve about 0.5 g manganese(II) sulphate in about 2 cm^3 of dilute sulphuric acid in a test-tube.
7. Carefully add about 10 drops concentrated sulphuric acid and cool the tube under a running tap.
8. Add a few drops of potassium manganate(VII) solution to obtain a deep red solution of Mn(III).
9. Dilute the red solution with about five times its volume of water, wait a few moments, and note any colour change.

Questions. Part B.

3. Explain what happened when the Mn(III) solution was diluted.

(Answer on page 83)

Procedure. Part C

Refer to your answer to Exercise 8, in which you predicted that it should also be possible to make Mn(III) from Mn(II) and Mn(IV).

10. In each of two test-tubes, dissolve a little manganese(II) sulphate in water and add an equal volume of sodium hydroxide solution to obtain a precipitate of manganese(II) hydroxide.

11. To one of the two tubes, add a little manganese(IV) oxide and stir.

12. Let both tubes stand for a few minutes, and note any changes.

Questions. Part C.

4. Can you see any sign of Mn(III) in the tubes?

5. What is different about the conditions of this experiment (part C) compared with the last (part B) which makes its success less likely?

6. What happens in the test-tube which had no manganese(IV) added? Suggest an explanation. (Hint: is the change greater in the upper part of the mixture?)

(Answers on page 83)

The method suggested in Exercise 9 for making Mn(V) was shown not to be worth trying, but your teacher may demonstrate another method.

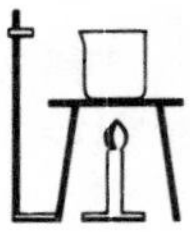

Similar interconversions from one oxidation state to another are possible for other transition elements, but we do not discuss these in detail. However, in the next exercise you apply some of what you have learned to the transition metal chromium.

Exercise 10

A

(a) Write down the electronic configuration (*s*, *p*, *d* electrons) of

(i) an atom of chromium, (ii) a chromium(II) ion.

(b) State the oxidation state (number) of chromium in

(i) $Cr_2O_7^{2-}$ (ii) CrO_4^{2-}

(c) Classify the following changes as oxidation, reduction and/or acid-base, giving a reason in each case.

(i) $Cr_2O_7^{2-} \rightarrow CrO_4^{2-}$* (ii) $Cr_2O_7^{2-} \rightarrow Cr^{3+}$

(d) By reference to standard electrode potentials, suggest three reagents which would effect the change in (c)(ii).

*Hint: what must be included to balance the equation?

(Answers on page 83)

Variable oxidation state is just one of the characteristics of transition elements. In the next section we look at a number of others, but all of them are related in some way to electron configuration and oxidation state.

CHARACTERISTICS OF TRANSITION ELEMENTS

You have probably studied transition elements briefly in your pre-A-level course and will be aware of some of their general characteristics. A more complete list is as follows:

1. Variable oxidation state.
2. Compounds are almost always coloured.
3. Complex ions are formed.
4. Catalysts almost always contain transition elements.
5. Paramagnetism is observed.
6. Physical properties, which make the elements useful as metals, are broadly similar.

Objectives. When you have finished this section you should be able to:

(8) list five general characteristics of transition elements in addition to variable oxidation state;

(9) relate these characteristics to electron arrangement;

(10) explain the terms complex ion, ligand and co-ordination number;

(11) name complex ions systematically given formulae;

(12) write formulae of complex ions given names;

(13) give examples of the use of transition elements or their compounds as catalysts.

Having discussed variable oxidation state in some detail, we now look briefly at each of the other general characteristics in turn in order to link them together. A more detailed study of some of these characteristics will appear in Level Two and Appendix Two.

Coloured compounds

You will have observed some of the striking colours of transition element compounds in Experiments 1 and 2. What may not yet be apparent is that virtually all compounds of transition elements are coloured. Also, few inorganic compounds of other elements are coloured, as you can confirm for yourself in the next exercise.

Exercise 11. Name one inorganic compound in common use which is coloured but does not contain a transition element.

(Answer on page 83)

Before we look for an explanation of the colour of these compounds, we will remind you of the reason for any coloured appearance.

In general, a substance appears coloured because it absorbs some of the light which falls on it. The light which is then reflected or transmitted to the observer's eye is not a complete spectrum of the wavelengths which make up white light, and appears to have a colour complementary to that of the absorbed light. For example, copper sulphate solution appears blue because it absorbs red light, as shown in Fig. 4.

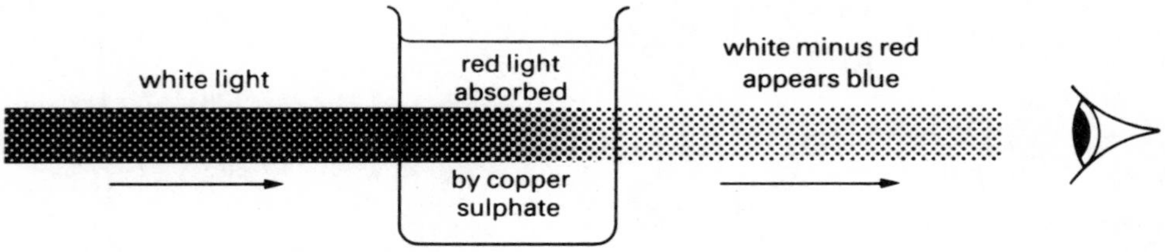

Fig.4.

All substances absorb some wavelengths of the electromagnetic spectrum in a variety of ways - this enables us to identify substances by infra-red and ultraviolet spectroscopy. However, the absorption of visible wavelengths always involves promotion of electrons from one energy level to another fairly close level, as shown in Fig. 5.

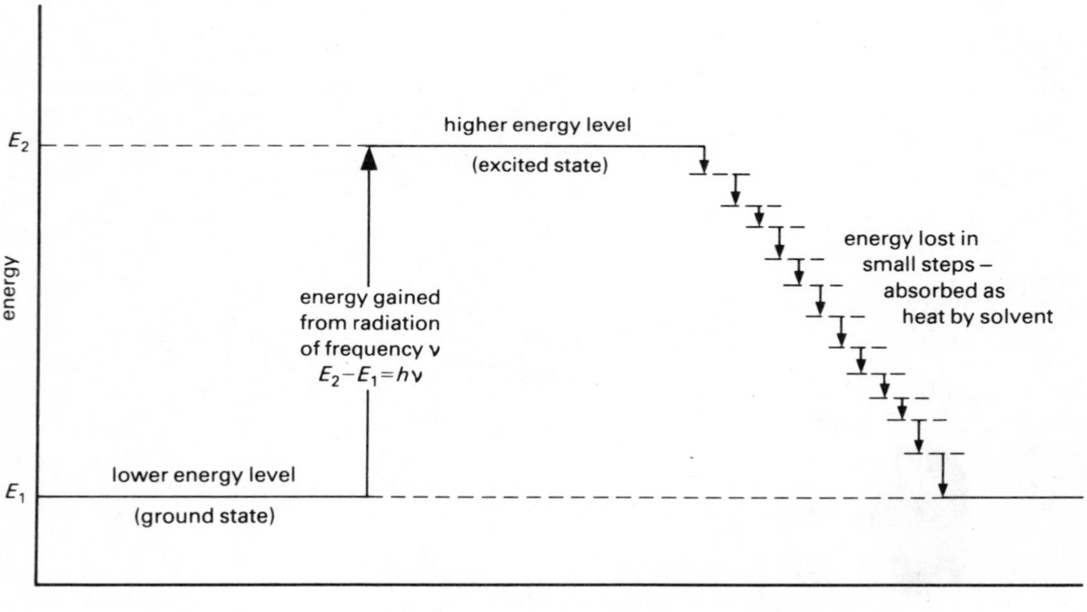

Fig.5.

Although the $3d$ and $4s$ levels are generally very close in compounds of transition metals, this is only a part of the reason for their colour, as you will see if you tackle Appendix Two. At this stage, it is sufficient for you to note that because of their particular electron configurations, compounds of transition elements have energy levels sufficiently close for them to absorb visible light.

Read about coloured compounds of transition elements before doing the next exercise. Your textbook may include an introductory account of the splitting of $3d$ energy levels, which you should find interesting although it is not likely to be examined.

Exercise 12 Why do you think that the following compounds are colourless - $ScCl_3$, $ZnSO_4$, $CuCl$?

(Answer on page 83)

A more detailed study of the electron transitions involved in the absorption of visible light appears in Appendix Two. Ask your teacher whether you should study it. Now we consider another of the general characteristics of transition elements.

Formation of complexes

Read the appropriate section of your textbook to find out what complex ions are, and how they are formed by transition elements. Make sure that you learn some examples of simple ligands, both charged and uncharged, and some examples of complex ions of different co-ordination number so that you can attempt the following exercises. You should also find out about the systematic naming of complex ions.

In your reading you may also find a treatment of the shapes of complex ions, their relative stabilities, and isomerism. We will deal with these aspects in Level Two.

Exercise 13 In the following complexes identify the central ion, the ligand(s) and the co-ordination number.

(a) $Cu(NH_3)_4{}^{2+}$ (c) $Co(OH)_2(H_2O)_4$

(b) $CrCl(H_2O)_5{}^{2+}$ (d) $(NH_4)_3VF_6$

(Answers on page 84)

Note that many texts enclose the formula of a complex ion in square brackets, e.g. $[Cu(NH_3)_4]^{2+}$. We do not follow this convention in this Unit to avoid confusion with the square brackets used for concentrations.

Exercise 14 Given the co-ordination numbers shown, write down the formulae and names of the complex ions formed between:

(a) Cu^{2+} and H_2O, (C.N. = 4)

(b) Fe^{3+} and CN^-, (C.N. = 6)

(c) Ni^{2+} and Cl^-, (C.N. = 4)

(d) Ag^+ and NH_3. (C.N. = 2)

(Answers on page 84)

Exercise 15 Identify four types of bonding in crystals of copper sulphate-5-water, $CuSO_4 \cdot 5H_2O$.

(Answer on page 84)

Now we take a brief look at the fourth and fifth items in our list of characteristics of transition elements.

Catalysis involving transition elements

You have learned in Unit P5 that a catalyst speeds up a chemical reaction by providing an alternative route with lower activation energy. Clearly, the catalyst must take part in the sequence of reactions, but since the eventual products are the same, the catalyst must be regenerated.

You study the mechanism of homogeneous catalysis in Level Two of this Unit, and you will find that this general characteristic of transition elements is also related to variable oxidation state. To emphasise the importance of transition elements in catalysis, try the next exercise.

Exercise 16 Write equations for at least six reactions in which a transition element (or compound) is used as a catalyst. At least four of these should be used in industry. Name the catalyst. (Hint: don't forget organic chemistry!)

(Answer on page 84)

Paramagnetism

Any substance which is attracted into a magnetic field is said to be paramagnetic, while if it is repelled it is diamagnetic. Transition elements and their ions are generally paramagnetic, whereas most others are diamagnetic.

Paramagnetism in transition elements is associated with unpaired electrons found in their partially-filled *d* orbitals. We will discuss this further in Appendix Two; ask your teacher whether you need to study it.

Note that ferromagnetism (which we usually refer to simply as 'magnetism') can be regarded as a very powerful paramagnetism and is confined to the elements iron, cobalt and nickel.

The last general characteristic of transition elements in our list is the broad similarity in physical and chemical properties. We look at this briefly here before going on to a more detailed study in subsequent sections.

Similar physical and chemical properties

It should be no surprise to find similar chemical properties, because chemical reactions always involve the outer electrons, and the atoms in each transition series have the same outermost electron shell (4*s*, 5*s*, or 6*s*), nearly always containing two electrons.

Physical properties also depend on the outer electrons (especially metallic conductivity), and also on the way electron arrangement determines atomic radius. Similar atomic radius generally gives rise to similar physical properties.

GENERAL PHYSICAL AND CHEMICAL PROPERTIES

Objectives. When you have finished this section you should be able to:

(14) relate physical properties of transition elements to electron arrangement and atomic radius;

(15) show how physical properties determine the practical uses of transition elements;

(16) give some examples of the chemical reactions of transition elements with air, water, acids and non-metals.

Similarity in physical properties

Earlier in the Unit (page 9), we stated that scandium and zinc are often not regarded as transition elements because their compounds do not have partially filled *d* orbitals.

Another reason for their exclusion is concerned with the physical properties of the elements, and you explore this in the next exercise.

Exercise 17 Look up the densities and melting-points of the elements from scandium to zinc. Suggest a reason for excluding scandium and zinc from the transition metals.

(Answer on page 84)

We confine our attention now to the first transition series from Ti to Cu, in which we examine trends in physical properties.

Use Table 3 to help you answer the following exercises.

Table 3

Property	Ti	V	Cr	Mn	Fe	Co	Ni	Cu
Metallic radius r_m/nm	0.145	0.132	0.137	0.137	0.124	0.125	0.125	0.128
Ionic radius (M^{2+}) r_i/nm	0.090	0.088	0.080	0.088	0.076	0.074	0.072	0.069
1st ionization energy/kJ mol^{-1}	660	650	650	720	760	760	740	750
Electronegativity (Pauling)	1.5	1.6	1.6	1.5	1.8	1.8	1.8	1.9

Exercise 18 Describe the general trends observed in Table 3 and explain them in terms of electron arrangement.

(Answer on page 84)

It is instructive to compare these trends with the trends in another horizontal row of elements in the Periodic Table, say those in Period 1 from Li to Ne. However, if you were asked to construct a table similar to Table 3 for Period 1, you would encounter difficulties with ionic radii, as you can see by reference to your data book.

Exercise 19 Why is it difficult to compare ionic radii of transition elements with those of Period 1 elements?

(Answer on page 84)

Nevertheless, a broad comparison can be made between transition elements and elements in a short period, and some firm conclusions drawn. Study your data book to help you do this in the next exercise.

Exercise 20 (a) How do the trends in radii, ionization energy, and electronegativity for the elements in a short period resemble the trends for transition elements?

(b) How do these trends differ?

(c) Explain the differences noted in (b) in terms of electron arrangement.

(Answers on page 84)

Just as ionization energy and electronegativity are related to atomic radius and electron arrangement, so are many other physical properties. You have touched on this relationship in Units I1 (*s*-Block Elements), I2 (The Halogens), I3 (The Periodic Table), S2 (Atomic Structure) and S4 (Bonding and Structure).

Exercise 21 For each of the following properties, briefly describe and explain how transition elements are broadly similar to one another and different from the *s*-block metals:

(a) density, (b) melting-point, (c) boiling-point.

(Answers on page **85**)

The physical properties of transition elements make them ideally suited for use as structural materials. We consider some of these uses in the next section.

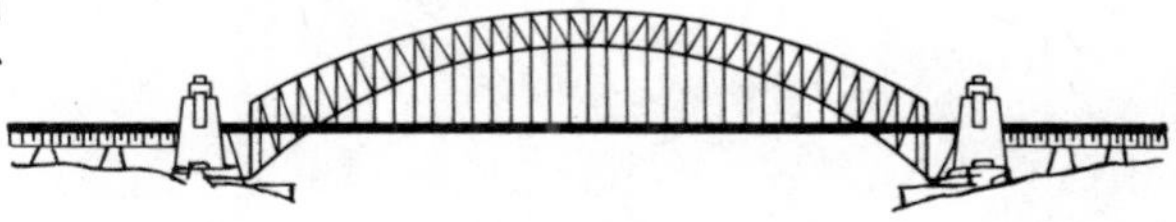

Transition elements as structural materials

Transition metals are often used as structural materials because they combine strength and durability with other desirable features such as electrical conductivity, ductility and pleasing appearance.

Read the section in your textbook dealing with the uses of transition metals, looking particularly for the reasons why titanium is used extensively in rocket technology. Also look for reasons why transition metals are used in alloys.

Fig.6. Space-shuttle launch from Cape Canaveral.

The most important example of a useful transition metal is, of course, iron. Its great advantage of being relatively cheap to produce outweighs its great disadvantage of suffering far worse corrosion than other more expensive transition metals. We consider the extraction of iron and the manufacture of steel in a later section, but it is relevant here to mention the incorporation of small amounts of other transition elements into alloy steels in order to modify their properties.

Ask your teacher whether you should study Ellingham diagrams in Appendix One (page 73) before going on to the following sections.

As well as the alloy steels, a number of other important alloys contain transition elements. Some of these are illustrated in Fig. 7, which is the subject of the next exercise.

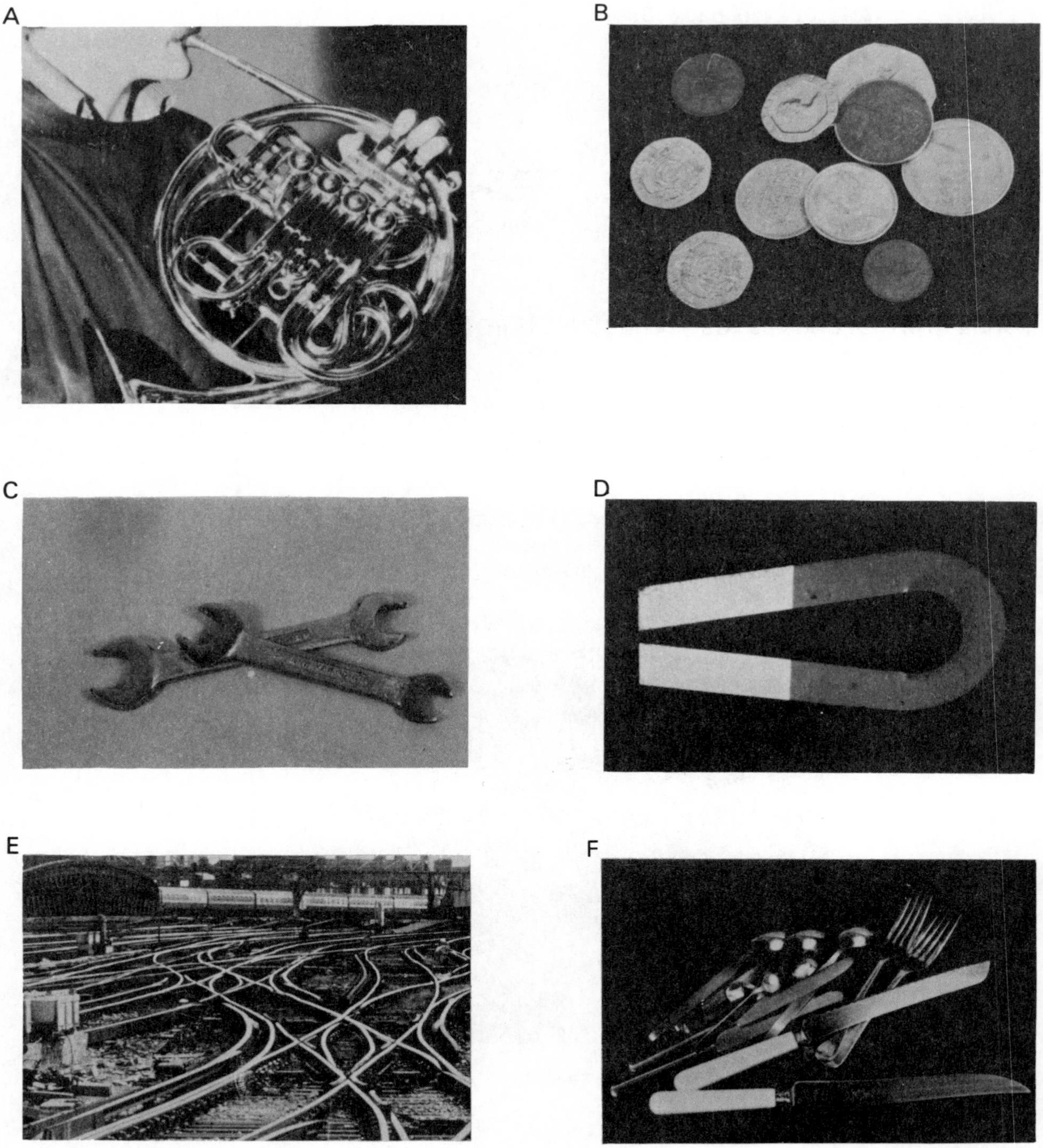

Fig.7. Some uses of alloys containing transition metals.

<u>Exercise 22</u> Name <u>two</u> transition elements used in each of the applications illustrated in Fig. 7.

(Answers on page 85)

The extensive use of transition elements in alloys is related to their atomic radii. You are asked about this in the next exercise.

Exercise 23 Why does the pattern of atomic radii of transition elements make them suitable for use in alloys?

(Answer on page 85)

To consolidate and organise what you have learned so far about the transition elements, attempt the following Teacher-marked Exercise. You may need to do some additional reading.

Teacher-marked Exercise Describe and explain how the following properties change along the first series of transition elements:

(a) atomic radius,

(b) maximum oxidation state,

(c) boiling-point,

(d) enthalpy of fusion.

As far as possible, relate your answers to the electronic structure of the elements and their bonding.

Having dealt with the physical properties of transition elements, we consider their chemical reactions.

Similarity in chemical properties

Instead of asking you to work through a long list of the reactions of individual elements, we simply note the following general statements. There are exceptions, of course, but the few you need to know are mentioned in the next exercise.

Transition elements generally:

1. react with non-oxidizing acids (e.g. dilute H_2SO_4, and HCl of any concentration) to give salts (commonly with the metal in the +2 oxidation state) and hydrogen;
2. react with oxidizing acids (e.g. concentrated H_2SO_4, and HNO_3 of any concentration) to give salts (sometimes with the metal in a higher oxidation state) and a gaseous reduction product of the acid (SO_2 or a mixture of oxides of nitrogen);
3. react with oxygen, the halogens and sulphur, to give a variety of oxides, halides and sulphides (refer to the oxidation states in Table 1 on page 9 for the most likely products);
4. are not attacked by water, but react at high temperatures with steam to give an oxide (lower oxidation state) and hydrogen;
5. have similar reactivities in the above reactions.

In the next exercise you apply these general statements to a few specific examples, and also recall some exceptions which you should already know about from your pre-A-level work. You should, of course refer to your textbook where necessary.

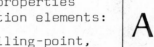

Exercise 24

(a) Name a transition element which does not react with non-oxidizing acids.

(b) Name a transition element which does not react with oxygen.

(c) Write equations for reactions between:

(i) manganese and dilute sulphuric acid,

(ii) nickel and concentrated sulphuric acid,

(iii) chromium and iodine,

(iv) chromium and fluorine,

(v) vanadium and oxygen,

(vi) titanium and sulphur.

(Answers on page 85)

In the next section we consider the extraction of iron from iron ore and the manufacture of steel. We do not deal with the extraction of other transition elements.

THE EXTRACTION OF IRON IN THE BLAST FURNACE

You have probably learned something of this process in your pre-A-level studies, in which case you may need only to revise your notes and add one or two further points. However, some syllabuses require you to discuss the process with reference to Ellingham diagrams relating free energy changes, $\Delta G^{\ominus}$, to temperature.

Ask your teacher whether you should study Ellingham diagrams in Appendix One (page 73) before going on to the following sections.

Fig.8. The base of a blast furnace in operation.

Objectives. When you have finished this section you should be able to:

(17) describe the reactions occurring in the operation of a blast furnace for the extraction of iron;

(18) state the chief impurities in cast iron and the effect of these on its properties.

Read about the blast-furnace in your textbook(s). Look for a set of simple equations for the relevant chemical reactions and the approximate temperatures of the regions of the furnace where these reactions occur. This will enable you to do the following exercises.

Exercise 25 Label a larger copy of Fig. 9 to show the following:

(a) the approximate dimensions,

(b) the hopper feed and its composition,

(c) the composition of the waste gases,

(d) the tuyères,

(e) the tapping-holes for molten iron and slag,

(f) the parts of the furnace where the temperatures are approximately 250 °C, 700 °C, 1150 °C and 1500 °C.

(g) equations for the main chemical reactions opposite the appropriate parts of the furnace. (Assume that the iron ore is mainly Fe_2O_3.)

(Answers on page 85)

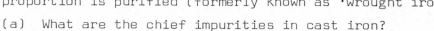

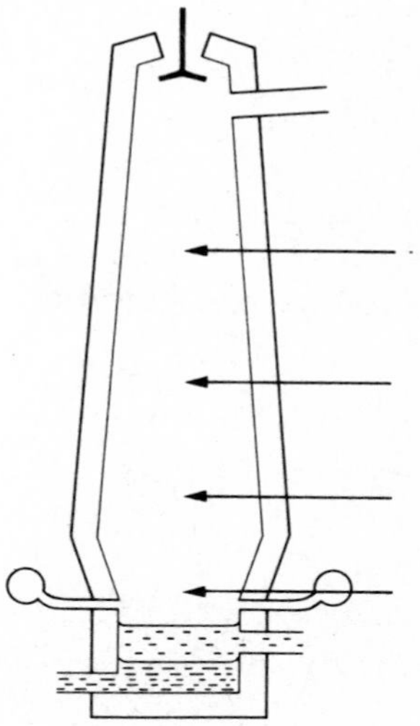

Fig.9. Extraction of iron in a blast furnace.

Exercise 26 Most of the iron produced by blast furnaces is made into steel, but some is used as 'cast iron' and a very small proportion is purified (formerly known as 'wrought iron').

(a) What are the chief impurities in cast iron?

(b) How do these impurities affect the properties of iron?

(c) State two uses of cast iron.

(Answers on page 86)

Exercise 27 (a) (i) Give the names and formulae of the iron compounds contained in two important iron ores.

A

(ii) Give the names of two impurities, commonly present in iron ores, which have to be removed in making iron and turning it into steel.

(b) (i) One of the substances fed into the blast furnace is there to remove an impurity or impurities. Give the name of this substance.

(ii) Write the equation(s) for a reaction between this substance and the impurity.

(iii) In what state does the impurity actually leave the furnace?

(c) Give the names of two substances which act as reducing agents in the blast furnace. In each case, give an equation showing its reducing action.

(d) Conditions are so arranged that the gases leaving the blast furnace will burn.

(i) What is the flammable gas?

(ii) Give one use for the emergent gases.

(e) Draw a labelled diagram of the apparatus you would use to prepare some anhydrous iron(III) chloride from iron.

(Answers on page **86**)

You have seen that cast iron is of limited use largely because of its high carbon content, which makes it brittle. Now we look briefly at the ways in which cast iron is made into steel of different types.

Steel production

There is a wide variety of different steels, all of which consist mostly of iron. However, their properties differ quite considerably due to the presence of small, carefully controlled proportions of elements such as carbon and other transition metals. Three steps may be involved in the making of a particular steel, the first being necessary in all cases.

1. Complete or partial removal of the impurities in cast iron.
2. Controlled addition of alloying elements.
3. Heat treatment.

Objective. When you have finished this section you should be able to:

(19) outline the production of steel from cast iron.

Read about steel production in a modern textbook. We suggest you focus your attention on the L.D. or Kaldo converters (based on the older Bessemer converter) rather than the open-hearth process, which is becoming much less important. Unless you are studying a metallurgy option (in which case your teacher will advise you) we suggest you need not learn details of percentage compositions or microstructures of different types of steel.

Fig.10. Casting steel.

The next exercise is about the main features of steel production.

Exercise 28 (a) What is the function of the oxygen which is blown through the impure iron obtained from the blast furnace?

(b) Why is oxygen preferred to air, which was formerly used in the older Bessemer converter?

(c) What is the composition of the lining of a converter and what is its function?

(d) What does the floating slag in a converter consist of, and under what circumstances is it used as a fertilizer (known to farmers as 'basic slag')?

(e) Outline what is meant by the term 'tempering of steel'.

(Answers on page 86)

LEVEL ONE CHECKLIST

You have now reached the end of Level One of this Unit. The following is a summary of the objectives in Level One. Read carefully through them and check that you have adequate notes. At this stage you should be able to:

(1) write electron configurations for the atoms of the first transition series from scandium to zinc;

(2) write electron configurations for some of the more common ions of transition elements;

(3) & (4) explain the general pattern of variable oxidation states in the transition elements;

(5) explain why scandium and zinc are often excluded from the study of transition elements;

(6) describe the preparation of a variety of oxidation states for vanadium and manganese;

(7) describe some examples of disproportionation and reverse disproportionation involving vanadium and manganese;

(8) list five general characteristics of transition elements in addition to variable oxidation state;

(9) relate these characteristics to electron arrangement;

(10) explain the terms complex ion, ligand and co-ordination number;

(11) & (12) name complex ions systematically given formulae and write formulae from names;

(13) give examples of the use of transition elements or their compounds as catalysts;

(14) relate physical properties of transition elements to electron arrangement and atomic radius;

(15) show how physical properties determine the practical uses of transition elements;

(16) give some examples of the chemical reactions of transition elements with air, water, acids and non-metals;

(17) describe the reactions occurring in the operation of a blast furnace for the extraction of iron;

(18) state the chief impurities in cast iron;

(19) outline the production of steel from cast iron.

LEVEL ONE TEST

To find out how well you have learned the material in Level One, try the test which follows. Read the notes below before starting.

1. You should spend about 1 hour on this test.

2. Hand your answers to your teacher for marking.

LEVEL ONE TEST

Questions 1-5 concern the preparation of a complex iron compound of formula $BaFeO_4$.

A solution of iron(III) nitrate in water is placed in a dropping funnel and added at the rate of 1 drop every 15 seconds to a boiling solution of sodium hydroxide in 2 M sodium chlorate(I) (sodium hypochlorite). The solution, which is purple in colour, is boiled for a minute or two and filtered into an aqueous solution of barium nitrate. The red precipitate of $BaFeO_4$ is filtered off and dried.

$$2Fe(NO_3)_3(aq) + 3NaOCl(aq) + 10NaOH(aq) \rightarrow 2Na_2FeO_4(aq) + 6NaNO_3(aq) + 5H_2O(l)$$

$$Na_2FeO_4(aq) + Ba(NO_3)_2(aq) \rightarrow BaFeO_4(s) + 2NaNO_3(aq)$$

A

1. The purple colour is most likely to be caused by

   A OCl^- B Fe^{3+} C FeO_4^{2-} D NO_3^- E Na^+ (1)

2. The most likely reason for using sodium chlorate(I) would be to

   A

   A act as an oxidizing agent

   B remove nitrate ions from solution

   C neutralize the sodium hydroxide

   D act as a reducing agent

   E buffer the solution (1)

3. If the iron(III) nitrate was added rapidly to a cold solution of alkaline sodium chlorate(I), the most likely result would be that

   A

   A the mixture would effervesce vigorously

   B a precipitate of sodium nitrate would form

   C the iron(III) ions would be converted into iron(II) ions

   D iron(III) hydroxide would precipitate

   E chlorine would be liberated (1)

4. The most suitable name for $BaFeO_4$ would be

   A

   A barium iron(II) oxide

   B barium iron(III) oxide

   C barium ferrate(III)

   D barium ferrate(IV)

   E barium ferrate(VI) (1)

5. In the first reaction, the sodium ions from the alkali are

   A

   A oxidized

   B unchanged

   C precipitated from solution

   D disproportionated

   E reduced (1)

In Questions 6 to 8 inclusive one, or more than one, of the suggested answers may be correct. You should answer as follows:

A if only 1, 2 and 3 are correct

B if only 1 and 3 are correct

C if only 2 and 4 are correct

D if only 4 is correct

E if some other response, or combination, is correct

6. Values for the standard electrode potentials ($E^\ominus$) of three systems are given below:

A

System	$E^\ominus$/V
$V^{3+}(aq) + e^- \rightarrow V^{2+}(aq)$	+0.20
$Fe^{3+}(aq) + e^- \rightarrow Fe^{2+}(aq)$	+0.77
$Fe^{3+}(aq) + 3e^- \rightarrow Fe(s)$	-0.04

If equal volumes of aqueous 1.0 M iron(III) and aqueous 1.0 M vanadium(II) are mixed

1 $Fe^{3+}(aq)$ is reduced to $Fe^{2+}(aq)$

2 $Fe^{3+}(aq)$ is reduced to Fe(s)

3 $V^{2+}(aq)$ is oxidized to $V^{3+}(aq)$

4 there is no reaction

(1)

7. The electronic configuration could represent

	3*d*					4*s*
Ar	↑↓	↑	↑	↑	↑	

A

1 Mn(II) 2 Fe(III) 3 Co(III) 4 Ni(II)

(1)

8. In which of the following is there an element with the same oxidation number as that of chromium in $K_2Cr_2O_7$?

A

1 Cl_2O_7 3 VO_2^+

2 $Fe(CN)_6^{4-}$ 4 K_2MnO_4

(1)

For Questions 9 and 10 choose an answer from A to E as follows:

A Both statements true: second explains first.

B Both statements true: second does <u>not</u> explain first.

C First true: second false.

D First false: second true.

E Both false.

	First statement	Second statement	
9.	In the ion $[Ni(H_2O)_6]^{2+}$ water is a bidentate ligand.	The oxygen atom in the water molecule has two lone pairs of electrons. (1)	A
10.	The gradation in properties along a series of transition elements is more marked than that along a period of non-transition elements.	Inner quantum levels are being filled with electrons along a series of transition elements.	A (1)

11. (a) State five properties which are typical of the transition elements and illustrate each with a specific example. (10)

A

(b) For each of the oxidation numbers +2, +3, +4, +6 and +7, write the formula of one compound or ion in which the transition element either chromium or manganese has that oxidation number. (5)

(c) For each of the five examples chosen in (b), name a reagent which will change the oxidation number and write the redox equation for the reaction. (10)

12. Cobalt, copper, iron and manganese are *d*-block elements.

A

(a) What is meant by the term '*d*-block element'? (2)

(b) Write the electronic configurations of Cu, Fe^{2+} and Mn^{2+}. (Use the symbol Ar followed by 'arrows-in-boxes' for the 3*d* and 4*s* orbitals.) (3)

(c) Explain in terms of their electronic configurations why Fe^{2+} ions are readily oxidized to Fe^{3+} ions, but Mn^{2+} ions are not readily oxidized to Mn^{3+} ions. (2)

(d) (i) Give the formula of a compound or ion containing manganese in an oxidation state of +7.

(ii) How do you account for the existence of the +7 oxidation state for manganese? (3)

(e) Cobalt forms a complex compound of formula $[Co(NH_3)_4Cl_2]^+ Cl^-$

(i) What is the oxidation state of cobalt in this compound?

(ii) Give the name of the complex ion contained in this compound.

(iii) How many moles of silver chloride would be immediately precipitated from one mole of this compound in aqueous solution by the addition of an excess of silver nitrate? (3)

Continued on next page.

13. (a) Describe qualitatively and explain the trend in atomic radius from titanium to copper.

(b) What bearing does this trend have on the use of the transition elements in alloys?

(c) Give two reasons why the metals potassium and copper have such widely different densitites and boiling-points. (4)

14. Write equations for the reactions between:

(a) vanadium and fluorine,

(b) cobalt and dilute hydrochloric acid,

(c) manganese and iodine,

(d) copper and concentrated sulphuric acid. (8)

(Total 60 marks)

LEVEL TWO

In Level Two we consider in more detail some of the characteristics of transition metals which you studied briefly in Level One. We begin with complex ions.

Formation and stability of complex ions

Most transition metal chemistry takes place in aqueous solution; we frequently refer to aqueous ions. However, when we write, say, $Cu^{2+}(aq)$ we refer not to simple Cu^{2+} ions surrounded by more or less mobile water molecules, but to the definite identifiable species $Cu(H_2O)_4{}^{2+}$. This is an example of a complex ion; the four molecules of water are ligands attached by dative covalent bonds, as shown below. This ion is surrounded by loosely-attached water molecules and is, therefore, best written as $Cu(H_2O)_4{}^{2+}(aq)$.

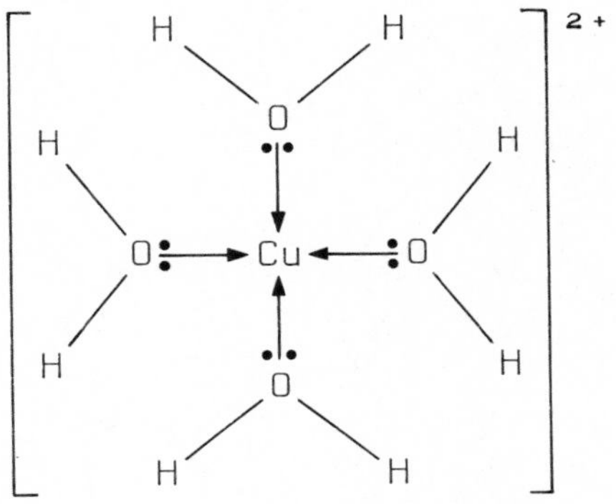

(Note that in some complex ions, the ligands are attached by ion-dipole bonds rather than dative covalent bonds, but we think the distinction is not important at A-level.)

In the formation of other complex ions, the water molecules are replaced by other ligands in equilibrium reactions such as:

$$Cu(H_2O)_4{}^{2+}(aq) + 4Cl^-(aq) \rightleftharpoons CuCl_4{}^{2-}(aq) + 4H_2O(l)$$

This equation is often simplified to:

$$Cu^{2+}(aq) + 4Cl^-(aq) \rightleftharpoons CuCl_4{}^{2-}(aq)$$

in just the same way as we often use $H^+(aq)$ to represent $H_3O^+(aq)$.

The equilibrium constants for reactions such as this are called stability constants, and you can apply to them what you learned about equilibrium constants in Unit P2 (Equilibrium I: Principles).

In the sections which follow, you learn how to use stability constants to predict ligand replacement reactions for various types of complex ions and how to compare stabilities experimentally. Also, we describe a practical use of complex ions in titrimetric analysis and, in order to make another link with work you have already done, we compare complex ion formation with acid-base reactions.

Stability constants

The term 'stability constant' is simply a special name given to an equilibrium constant applied to the formation of a complex ion, e.g.

$$Cu^{2+}(aq) + 4Cl^{-}(aq) \rightleftharpoons CuCl_4^{2-}(aq)$$

$$K_{st} = \frac{[CuCl_4^{2-}(aq)]}{[Cu^{2+}(aq)]\,[Cl^{-}(aq)]^4}$$

Objectives. When you have finished this section, you should be able to:

(20) use the equilibrium law to write expressions for stability constants of complex ions;

(21) use stability constants in simple calculations.

Read the section in your textbook which deals with the formation of complexes, looking for references to equilibrium and stability constants, so that you can attempt the exercises which follow. Some textbooks do not refer to stability constants by name. If you cannot find an account, all you need is to recall the equilibrium law and apply it to the appropriate equations.

Exercise 29 (a) What is the name of the ion $CuCl_4^{2-}$?

(b) The formation of the $CuCl_4^{2-}$ ion, summarised in the equation above, takes place in four stages, the water molecules being replaced one by one. For each stage, write an equation and an expression for the stability constant.

(c) Show that the product of the four intermediate stability constants is equal to the overall stability constant obtained directly from the overall equation.

(d) What is the unit of the overall stability constant?

(Answers on page **86**)

Note that overall stability constants are the ones most often used, since the ligand is usually in excess.

Exercise 30 The stability constant of the dicyanoargentate(I) ion is 1.0×10^{21} mol^{-2} dm^{6}. Explain what is meant by this statement, including an equation in your answer.

(Answer on page **87**)

Exercise 31 What is the concentration of silver ions in a solution where the concentrations of cyanide ions and dicyanoargentate(I) ions are 0.50 mol dm^{-3} and 0.10 mol dm^{-3} respectively?

(Answer on page **87**)

An application of complex ion chemistry

When articles are plated with silver or gold, it is necessary to have a very low concentration of metal ions in the electrolyte in order to achieve even plating which adheres well, but there must also be a substantial 'reserve' of metal ions so that an adequate amount of metal can be deposited on the cathode. These requirements are met by complexing the metal ions with added cyanide ions. As plating proceeds, the silver ions removed from solution are replaced by disturbing the equilibrium:

$$Ag(H_2O)_2^+(aq) + 2CN^-(aq) \rightleftharpoons Ag(CN)_2^-(aq) + 2H_2O(aq)$$

Silver ions are also replenished by the dissolving of a silver anode, but these are not immediately available at the cathode. The complex ion acts as a 'carrier' of silver between anode and cathode.

The replacement (or displacement) of ligands in the formation of a complex ion can also be regarded as a competition for the cation between the two ligands. In this way, the formation of a complex ion is similar to an acid-base reaction in which two bases compete for a proton, as we now show.

Competition for cations

When more than one ligand is available in excess for bonding to a transition metal ion, one product will predominate, depending on the relative stability constants.

There is a competition between the ligands for the cation somewhat similar to the competition for a proton between two bases. In the simplest examples of competition, one of the two competing species is water. For example,

H^+ $\qquad$ H^+

$$CH_3CO_2H(aq) + H_2O(l) \rightleftharpoons CH_3CO_2^-(aq) + H_3O^+(aq)$$

acid $\qquad$ base $\qquad$ base $\qquad$ acid

Cu^{2+} $\qquad$ Cu^{2+}

$$Cu(H_2O)_4^{2+}(aq) + 4Cl^-(aq) \rightleftharpoons 4H_2O(l) + CuCl_4^-(aq)$$

complex $\qquad$ ligand $\qquad$ ligand $\qquad$ complex

In the first reaction above, $CH_3CO_2^-$ is a stronger base (has a greater affinity for H^+) than H_2O so that the equilibrium lies toward the left. The equilibrium constant, here called the dissociation constant, is very small.

In the second reaction, the Cl^- ion has a greater affinity for Cu^{2+} than has H_2O. The equilibrium constant, here called a stability constant, is large.

We now move to the study of some other, less simple, ligands.

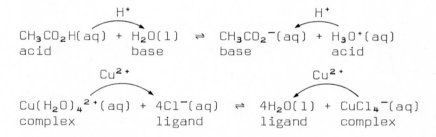

Polydentate ligands

These are ligands with more than one site for dative covalent bonding.

Objectives. When you have finished this section you should be able to:

(22) explain the terms polydentate and chelate;

(23) explain why polydentate ligands generally give very stable complex ions.

Read again the section in your textbook on complex ions, looking particularly for the meanings of the terms 'polydentate' and 'chelate'. This will help you to do the following exercises.

Exercise 32   Name the ligand $H_2NCH_2CH_2NH_2$ and state how many bonds you would expect it to make with a central cation. Explain your choice.

(Answer on page **87**)

A very useful hexadentate ligand is the ion formed from bis(bis(carboxymethyl)-amino)ethane.

You may be pleased to know that this very clumsy (but very informative) name is rarely used. The ion is known as edta, which is the abbreviation for the traditional name ethylene-diamine-tetra-acetate and its formula is shown below. The parent acid can be written as H_4edta, although you may find reference to EDTA! (This is just one of the hazards of studying chemistry at a time when the use of systematic and recommended nomenclature is not universal!)

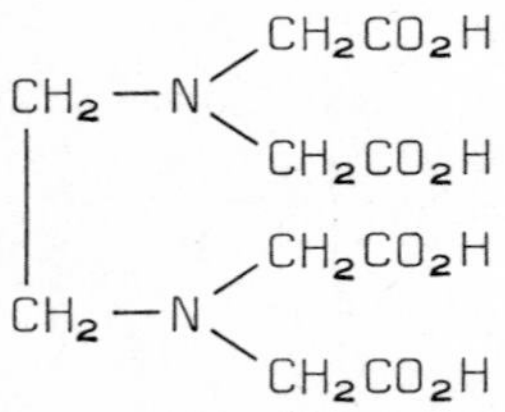

$$CH_2-N\begin{cases}CH_2CO_2H\\CH_2CO_2H\end{cases}$$
$$CH_2-N\begin{cases}CH_2CO_2H\\CH_2CO_2H\end{cases}$$
$$H_4edta$$

$$CH_2-N\begin{cases}CH_2CO_2{}^-\\CH_2CO_2{}^-\end{cases}$$
$$CH_2-N\begin{cases}CH_2CO_2{}^-\\CH_2CO_2{}^-\end{cases}$$
$$edta$$

The carboxylic acid group is often encountered in ligands but it is usually the ion rather than the acid which is involved in bonding and only one of the two oxygen atoms forms bonds. You explore this in the next exercise, which uses edta as an example.

To do this exercise, you should first construct a model of the edta ligand from the structural formula given, using a 'ball and spoke' model kit. You need one sphere with six evenly spaced holes to represent the central cation.

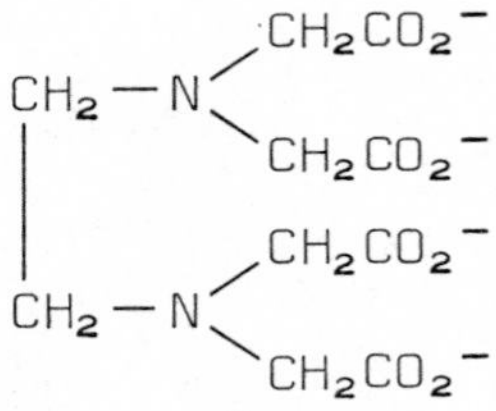

Exercise 33 (a) Which atoms in an edta ion might be able to form dative bonds? Does your answer explain why edta is described as being hexadentate?

(b) Suggest reasons

(i) why it is the ion rather than the acid which is involved in bonding,

(ii) why only one of the two oxygen atoms in each carboxyl group forms bonds.

(c) Suggest a reason why polydentate ligands generally give more stable complexes than monodentate ligands.

(Answers on page 87)

Now that you have encountered a variety of ligands, you study how stability constants vary with the nature of the ligand.

Relative stabilities of complex ions

You investigate the relative stabilities of complexes formed from various ligands in a series of short experiments, but to help you predict what will happen you should first do the next exercise.

Exercise 34 The stability constants of two complex ions are:

$Cu(NH_3)_4^{2+}$: $K_{st} = 1.58 \times 10^{13}\ mol^{-4}\ dm^{12}$

$CuCl_4^{2-}$: $K_{st} = 3.98 \times 10^{5}\ mol^{-4}\ dm^{12}$

(a) Write the equations to which these constants refer.

(b) Use the equations and stability constants to predict what would happen if ammonia solution were added drop by drop to a solution of $CuCl_4^{2-}$ ions.

(Answers on page 88)

Now you should be ready for the next experiment, which illustrates the relative stabilities of some complex ions. If your laboratory time is limited, you should make the predictions in Results Table 3 before you reach the laboratory.

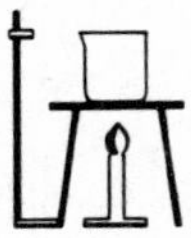

EXPERIMENT 3

Relative stabilities of some complex ions

Aim

The purpose of this experiment is to test predictions of ligand replacement reactions made using stability constants.

Introduction

In a series of test-tube reactions you examine a number of ligand replacement reactions. One type, in which charged and uncharged ligands are represented as lig^- and LIG respectively, can be represented:

$$Cu(LIG)_4^{2+} + 4\ lig^- \rightleftharpoons Cu(lig)_4^{2-} + 4\ LIG$$

You use stability constants to predict the outcome before mixing suitable pairs of solutions.

Requirements

6 test-tubes
test-tube rack
copper(II) sulphate solution, 0.20 M $CuSO_4$
wash-bottle of distilled water
sodium chloride solution, saturated NaCl
sodium ethanedioate solution, 0.20 M $(CO_2Na)_2$ (sodium oxalate)
1,2-diaminoethane solution, 0.10 M $(CH_2NH_2)_2$
edta solution (sodium salt), 0.10 M $C_{10}H_{14}O_8N_2Na_2$

Procedure

1. Complete the four prediction columns (headed 'P') in a copy of Results Table 3, using the stability constants given. Use a '√' to indicate 'replacement' and a 'x' to indicate 'no reaction'.
2. Place about 1 cm^3 of copper sulphate solution in each of five test-tubes.
3. To the first tube add about 5 cm^3 distilled water. This tube is for colour comparison with the others.
4. To the second tube add about 5 cm^3 sodium chloride solution a little at at time, noting any colour changes.
5. To the third tube add about 5 cm^3 sodium ethanedioate in the same way.
6. Similarly, to the fourth and fifth tubes add diaminoethane and edta solutions respectively.
7. The colours in the five tubes are predominantly due to the five complex ions shown in Results Table 3. Write down the colours in your table, and fill in the first results column (headed 'R'). Again, use a '√' or a 'x' to show whether or not replacement of ligands has occurred.

Note that, in addition to the abbreviation edta, we use 'ox' to represent the ethanedioate (oxalate) ligand and 'en' to represent the 1,2-diaminoethane ligand (ethylenediamine)

Results Table 3

Ligand	H_2O		Cl^-		$C_2O_4^{2-}$ = ox		$NH_2C_2H_4NH_2$ = en		$C_{10}H_{14}O_8N_2^{4-}$ = edta	
Complex ion	$Cu(H_2O)_4^{2+}$		$CuCl_4^{2-}$		$Cu(ox)_2^{2-}$		$Cu(en)_2^{2+}$		$Cu(edta)^{2-}$	
Colour	clear blue		lime green		sky blue		purple		see blue	
Stability constant	———		4.0×10^5 $mol^4\ dm^{-12}$		2.1×10^{10} $mol^2\ dm^{-6}$		———		6.3×10^{18} $mol\ dm^{-3}$	
	Predictions (P) and results (R). ✓ = replacement, x = none									
Test	P	R	P	R	P	R	P	R	P	R
Add H_2O			✓	✓	✓	✗		✗		✗
Add Cl^-	✓	✓			✗	✗		✗		✗
Add ox	✓	✓	✓	✓				✗		✗
Add en	✓	✓	✓	✓	✓	✓				✗
Add edta	✓	✓	✓	✓	✓	✓		✓		

(Specimen results on page 87)

8. Divide the solution containing $CuCl_4^{2-}$ ions into four parts. To each of these add an excess of one of the other four ligands in turn - use the original ligand solutions and not the complex ion solutions you have made. Complete the second results column according to whether or not you think replacement has occurred.

9. Repeat step 8 for the remaining complex ion solutions and complete the remaining results columns.

Questions

1. Could you have made any tentative predictions without knowing stability constants?

2. Estimate the approximate stability constant for $Cu(en)_2^{2+}$.

3. One of the ligand exchange reactions appeared to be readily reversible. Which one was this?

4. Calculate the ratio $[Cu(H_2O)_4^{2+}(aq)]/[CuCl_4^{2-}(aq)]$ for the following values of $[Cl^-(aq)]$:

   (a) 5.0 mol dm^{-3} (in saturated NaCl)

   (b) 0.050 mol dm^{-3} (in dilute NaCl).

   How do these ratios help to explain the reversible nature of the ligand exchange?

(Answers on page 87)

The ion edta forms very stable complexes with many other metal ions as well as copper. We now consider an application of this fact.

Use of edta in titrations

Objective. When you have finished this section you should be able to:

(24) explain the use of complexes in titrimetric analysis.

Edta forms such stable complexes with many metal ions that the reactions can be used in titrations to measure their concentrations. Another complex, less stable but more highly coloured, is used as an indicator. This is simply an application of the exchange of ligands you have just studied, as you will see in the next exercise.

Exercise 35 25.0 cm^3 of an orange solution of Fe^{3+} ions of unknown concentration was titrated with 0.10 M edta, using a little 2-hydroxybenzoic acid as an indicator. When 20.0 cm^3 of edta solution had been added, the violet colour of the 2-hydroxybenzoate complex disappeared, leaving a clear yellow solution.

(a) Explain the colour changes.

(b) Assuming the complex ion formed to be $Fe(edta)^-$, write an equation for its formation.

(c) Calculate the concentration of Fe^{3+} ions in the original solution.

(Answers on page 88)

Having considered stability constants and the relative stabilities of various complex ions, we now move on to consider their shapes.

SHAPES OF COMPLEX IONS AND ISOMERISM

You have learned that co-ordination numbers 2, 4 and 6 are common in complex ions. These co-ordination numbers are associated with different three-dimensional shapes, and consideration of these shapes in this section leads you to study how the various types of isomerism you have met in organic chemistry can also arise in inorganic chemistry.

Objectives. When you have finished this section you should be able to:

(25) describe shapes commonly adopted by complex ions;

(26) explain how structural, geometric and optical isomerism can arise in complexes, giving examples.

Read the section on shapes of complex ions in your textbook(s) and use it to do the next exercise.

Exercise 36 What four shapes are commonly adopted by complex ions of coordination numbers 2, 4 and 6? Give an example of each.

(Answer on page 88)

Most of your work on isomerism concerns organic compounds, and you have learned about the main types of isomerism in Unit O3 (More Functional Groups). Both structural isomerism and stereoisomerism occur in inorganic chemistry as well, particularly in complexes, but there are fewer subdivisions. The main differences between organic and inorganic isomerism are as follows.

Differences between organic and inorganic isomerism

1. Inorganic structural isomerism is simpler; there are no subdivisions (chain-branch, positional, functional group, metamerism).
2. Inorganic optical isomerism is not concerned with asymmetric carbon atoms. Occasionally, there may be some other tetrahedral chiral centre but, more often, optical isomerism arises from the different ways of attaching bidentate ligands in octahedral complexes.
3. Inorganic geometrical isomers do not usually arise from different arrangements around a double bond. However, the prefixes *cis*- and *trans*- are used, but with reference to some other structural feature.

Read the section on isomerism in complexes in your textbook(s). Look for examples of structural isomerism, optical isomerism and *cis-trans*-isomerism (or geometrical isomerism). You should then be able to do the following exercises.

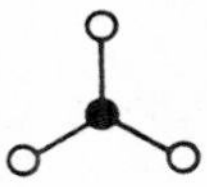

You may be able to manage without making models of complexes for some of the exercises, but you will certainly need them sooner or later. You can use the same 'ball and spoke' type that is so useful in organic chemistry, but a simpler type, using coloured plastic tubing (like drinking straws), is particularly suited to complex ion isomerism (see Fig. 11). Whichever type of model you use, you must be able to represent a central atom forming six evenly-spaced bonds (in octahedral directions).

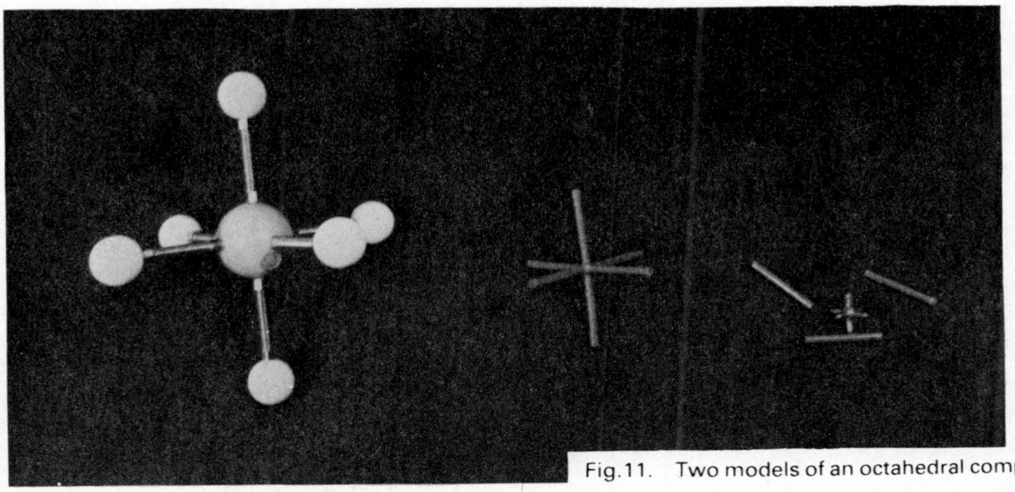

Fig.11. Two models of an octahedral complex.

Exercise 37 There are two isomers with the formula $Cr(H_2O)_5ClBr$.

(a) Identify the two different complex ions in these compounds.

(b) What shape do these ions have?

(c) What type of isomerism is this?

(Answers on page **88**)

Exercise 38 When hydrogen chloride is passed into cold chromium(III) nitrate solution, violet crystals A, $CrCl_3 \cdot 6H_2O$, are obtained. These lose no water when stood over concentrated sulphuric acid in a desiccator, and 1 mol of A gives 3 mol of AgCl immediately, on addition of silver nitrate to the solution. Measurements of the electrical conductivity suggest that each 'molecule' of A gives four ions in solution.

On cooling a hot solution of chromium(III) chloride, green crystals B, $CrCl_3 \cdot 6H_2O$, are formed. B loses water over concentrated sulphuric acid to give $CrCl_3 \cdot 4H_2O$.

On addition of silver nitrate, 1 mol of B gives 1 mol of AgCl at once. Another 2 mol of AgCl are slowly formed, and the colour of the solution changes at the same time. Conductivity measurements suggest that each 'molecule' of B gives two ions.

By treatment of a solution of B successively with sulphuric and hydrochloric acids, the green crystals C, also with the formula $CrCl_3 \cdot 6H_2O$, can be made. 1 mol of C loses 1 mol of water over concentrated sulphuric acid, gives 2 mol of AgCl at once and another 1 mol more slowly, and has a conductivity corresponding to the formation of three ions in solution.

(a) Suggest structures for compounds A, B and C. Give reasons.

(b) Suggest a structure for yet another compound with the formula $CrCl_3 \cdot 6H_2O$. What would be its behaviour with silver nitrate and with concentrated sulphuric acid? What kind of electrical conductivity would it have?

(Answers on page **89**)

Exercise 39 The compound $Co(NH_3)_3(NO_2)_2Cl$ is soluble in water, and has two possible structures:

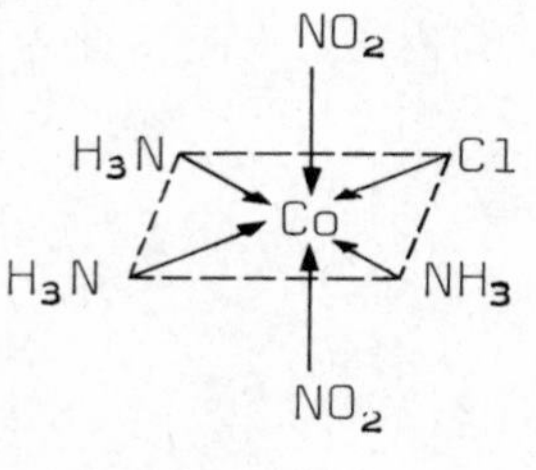

A

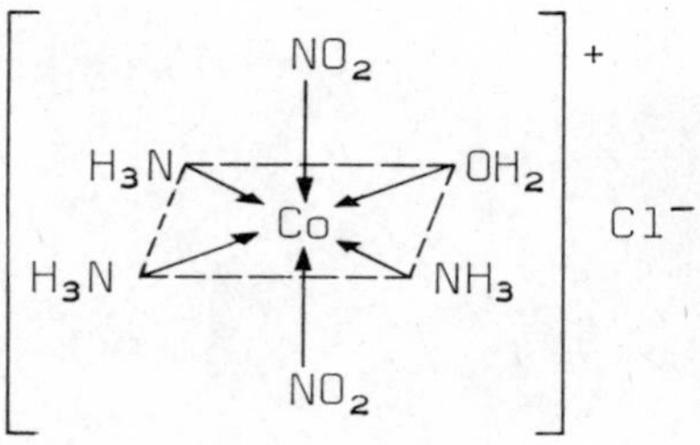

B

(a) How would you show that B, and not A, is the correct structure?

(b) How would you find out if there is an equilibrium between B and A in the solution?

(Answers on page **89**)

Exercise 40 How many isomeric ions are there with the formula $Co(NH_3)_4Cl_2^+$? Sketch them using the outline shown.

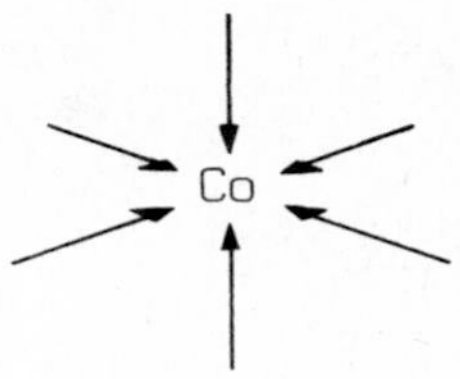

(Answer on page 89)

You should now be clear about structural and geometric isomerism in transition element compounds. We move on to discuss optical isomerism in more detail.

Optical isomerism

Examples of optical isomerism you have met in organic chemistry have always been concerned with an 'asymmetric carbon atom' (or more than one), i.e. a carbon atom attached by four tetrahedrally-directed bonds to four different atoms or groups.

The parallel situation, where four different ligands are attached tetrahedrally to a transition metal ion, is rarely encountered. However, asymmetry frequently arises in octahedral complexes containing bidentate ligands, and we now consider some examples.

Although the geometry is not quite so simple as in tetrahedral asymmetry, the principle of left-handedness and right-handedness (or mirror-image isomerism) still applies, as we show in the next exercise. In order to do the exercise, you need a molecular model kit with at least two atoms which can make six bonds each in octahedral directions and, if possible, a small mirror.

First, make a model of the chromium(III) complex ion shown in Fig. 12. This complex has four monodentate ligands (NH_3) and one bidentate ligand ($H_2NCH_2CH_2NH_2$). As you saw in Experiment 3, we can represent this ligand by the symbol 'en', both in the diagram and in the formula, $Cr(NH_3)_4en^{3+}$. If you have the appropriate type of model kit, you can represent the bidentate ligand by one piece of tube bent back on itself.

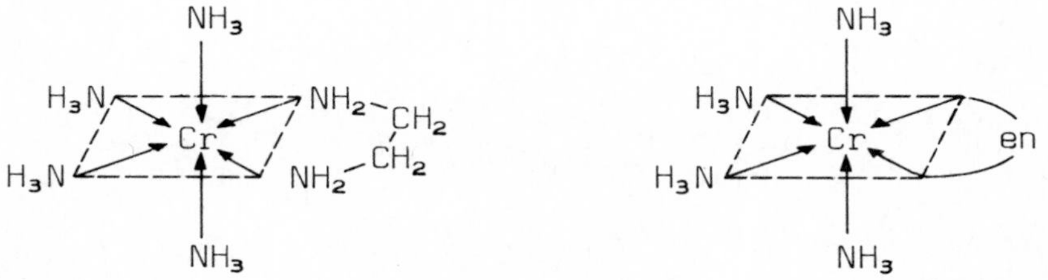

Fig.12.

Note that, for simplicity, we have not included the overall charge in the diagrams.

Now use your model, and adaptations of it, to do the following exercise.

Exercise 41 (a) Is the ion $Cr(NH_3)_4en^{3+}$ optically active? If necessary, make another model and use a mirror.

(b) Make models of the geometric isomers of $Cr(NH_3)_2(en)_2^{3+}$ by exchanging two NH_3 ligands for one 'en' ligand. Sketch them in a similar way to Fig. 12. Are they optically active? How many isomers of $Cr(NH_3)_2(en)_2^{3+}$ are there in all?

(c) Make models of the isomers of $Cr(en)_3^{3+}$ and sketch them. State the type of isomerism.

(Answers on page 89)

In order to help you consolidate the work you have done, look at the section on complex ions in the ILPAC video-programme 'The Transition Metals', if it is available.

Now we consider how the formulae of complex ions can be determined.

STOICHIOMETRY OF COMPLEX IONS

It should be clear to you by now that large numbers of different complexes can be formed from any one transition metal ion, and you may well wonder how their structures have been determined and how they can be distinguished from one another.

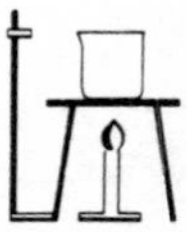

We do not pursue this matter in great detail at A-level but we can easily make a start by considering how the formula of a complex ion can be determined. This is the subject of the next experiment, in which you use a colorimeter. We give full details of the operation of this instrument, although you may already have used one in Unit P5 (Chemical Kinetics).

Objective. When you have finished this section you should be able to:

(27) describe how the formula of a complex ion can be determined by colorimetry.

EXPERIMENT 4

Determining the formula of a complex ion

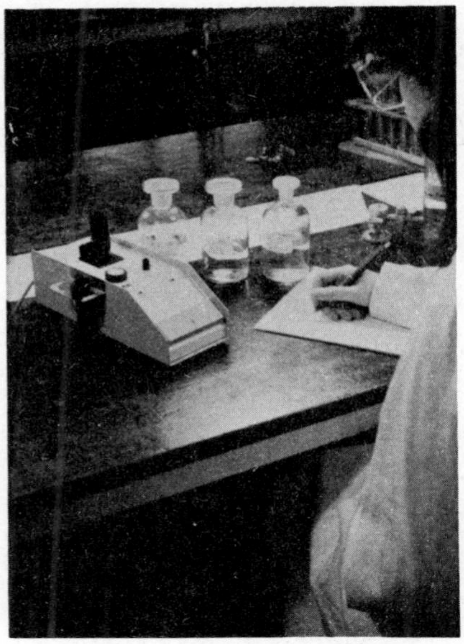

Aim

The purpose of this experiment is to use colorimetry to find the formula of the complex ion formed from copper(II) ions and ammonia. The same method can be used for many other complex ions.

Introduction

Using different proportions of copper(II) ion and ammonia you prepare mixtures and examine them in a colorimeter. The mixture which shows the most intense colour (and, therefore, the greatest absorbance) indicates the proportions of Cu^{2+} and NH_3 in the complex ion.

Requirements

safety spectacles
3 beakers, 100 cm^3
3 burettes, 50 cm^3 or 3 graduated pipettes, 10 cm^3
3 small funnels for filling burettes
8 test-tubes, to fit colorimeter
8 corks or bungs to fit test-tubes
test-tube rack
ammonium sulphate solution, 2.0 M $(NH_4)_2SO_4$
copper(II) sulphate solution, 0.10 M $CuSO_4$
ammonia solution, 0.10 M NH_3
colorimeter, with filters

Procedure

1. Prepare a different mixture in each of 8 test-tubes by running in from burettes or graduated pipettes the volumes of the three solutions shown in Results Table 4. Cork each tube and shake to mix thoroughly.

Results Table 4

Tube number	1	2	3	4	5	6	7	8
Volume of $(NH_4)_2SO_4/cm^3$	15	5	5	5	5	5	5	5
Volume of $CuSO_4/cm^3$	0.0	1.0	1.5	2.0	2.5	3.0	4.0	5.0
Volume of NH_3/cm^3	0.0	9.0	8.5	8.0	7.5	7.0	6.0	5.0
Colorimeter reading	0.0							

(Specimen results on page 90)

2. Choose a suitable filter for this experiment. If you are not quite sure which filter to use, look at the notes at the end of this procedure section.

3. With the filter in position, put tube 1 into the colorimeter, cover it to exclude stray light, and turn the adjusting knob so that the meter shows zero absorbance (or, on some colorimeters, 100% transmission).

Ideally, this should set the intensity of the light reaching the tubes for the whole experiment but, because simple colorimeters tend to give a light intensity which is not constant, you should repeat this step immediately before each reading you take.

4. Still with tube 1 in the colorimeter, check for constancy of meter reading with the tube rotated and moved to slightly different positions. Mark the tube so that you can replace it in such a way as to get the same reading each time.

If necessary, change the tube until you are satisfied. (With some of the simplest colorimeters, it may not be possible for you to be too fussy!)

5. Immediately after setting zero with tube 1, replace it with tube 2 and take a reading of absorbance (or % transmission). To minimise errors due to irregular tube diameter and position, rotate the tube and take an average reading. (If you are lucky enough to be using matched tubes, put the mark in the same position each time.)

Also, check the zero again after the reading and repeat if necessary. Record the average reading in a copy of Results Table 4.

6. Repeat steps 3 and 4 before taking further colorimeter readings for each of the remaining coloured solutions in turn.

7. Plot a graph of meter reading against volume of reactants as shown in Fig. 13. If your meter shows absorbance, the graph will show a peak; if it shows transmittance, the graph will show a trough.

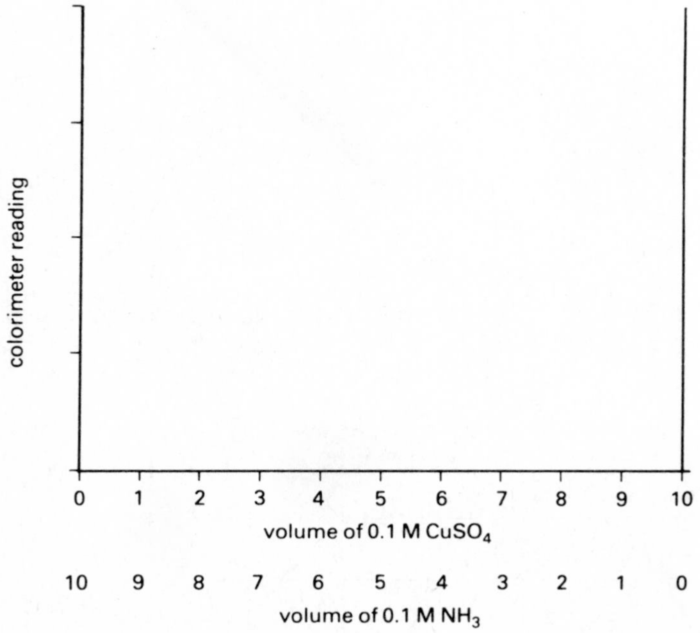

Fig. 13.

8. From the graph, determine the volumes of $CuSO_4$ and NH_3 corresponding to the peak (or trough if you are working with transmittance). These volumes may not necessarily be those used in any of the tubes, but should give a simple whole number ratio.

9. Use the simple whole number ratio obtained from the graph to write the formula for the complex ion.

Choosing a filter

Ideally, the filter lets through only light of the particular wavelength which is absorbed by the complex ion. So for a blue complex ion, which absorbs yellow light, you need a yellow filter - yellow is the complementary colour to blue. See Fig. 14.

If you are not clear which filter has the complementary colour of the solution you are using, then follow the detailed procedure below.

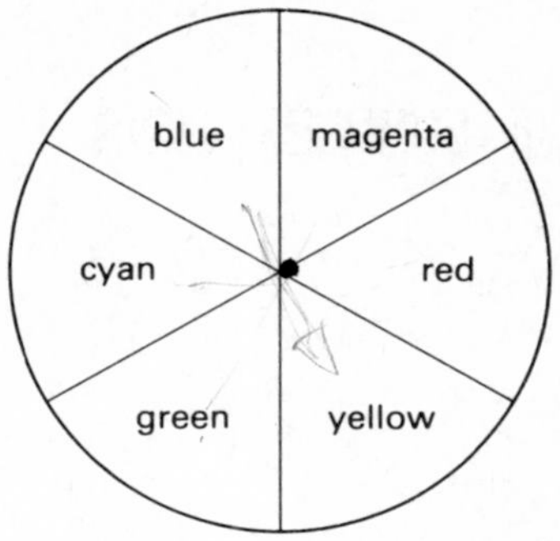

Fig.14.

1. Put any one of the available filters into the slot in the colorimeter, and insert tube 1, covering it to exclude stray light. Turn the adjusting knob so that the meter shows zero absorbance (or, on some colorimeters, 100% transmission). Mark the rim of the tube so that you can replace it in the same position.
2. Replace tube 1 with tube 5 and take a reading of absorbance (or of % transmission). Mark this tube too so that you can replace it in the same position.
3. Repeat steps 1 and 2 above for all the filters in turn.
4. Choose the filter which gives the greatest absorbance (or least transmission) and go back to step 3 of the procedure section.

Questions

1. What is the function of the ammonium sulphate in this experiment? If you do not know the answer, try adding ammonia solution to copper sulphate solution without any ammonium sulphate present. If you are not in the laboratory, or if you still need a clue, look up your notes on the common ion effect - Unit P2 (Equilibrium I: Principles).
2. Why does the absorbance decrease after the peak while the amount of added copper ions increases?
3. Why does the absorbance increase up to the peak while the amount of added ammonia decreases?
4. How would your results be affected by using the wrong filter?
5. How would your results be affected by using no filter at all?

(Answers on page 90)

Extension

The method described above can be used with very little modification (if any) to find the formulae for many other complex ions. You may wish to try, for example, using a solution of diaminoethane (ethylenediamine) in place of the ammonia in Experiment 4. If you do this, the ammonium sulphate is not necessary and should be replaced with water.

Other complexes you might try are those made from:

nickel(II) ions and edta

iron(III) ions and thiocyanate ions

Note that the volumes given in Results Table 4 may need adjusting for different complexes. Ask your teacher for advice.

Now we move on to consider another aspect of the chemistry of complex ions.

ACIDITY OF COMPLEX IONS

Solutions of some complex ions, particularly the aqua-complexes, are found to be definitely acidic. The extent of this acidity varies with the nature and charge of the central ion.

Objectives. When you have finished this section you should be able to:

(28) explain why solutions of some complex ions are acidic;

(29) recognise that pH often affects redox potentials.

You study this acidity in a revealing exercise, in which you apply what you have already learned about acids and about polarization of ions. This exercise concerns the ion $Fe(H_2O)_6{}^{3+}$ but the principles apply also to other ions.

1. A solution of iron(III) chloride has a pH of 4.0. What ions must be present, and in what concentration, to give the solution this pH?

A1. Hydrogen ions must be present, in concentration 1.0×10^{-4} mol dm^{-3}.

Q2. What is the source of these hydrogen ions?

A2. The hydrogen ions must come from the water.

Q3. Since pure water has a pH of 7, the low pH of the solution must be due to interaction of water molecules with Fe^{3+} ions and/or Cl^- ions.

What should lead you to expect more interaction with Fe^{3+} ions than with Cl^- ions?

A3. The greater charge on Fe^{3+} ion attracts polar water molecules more strongly than Cl^- ion. As you have seen, this leads to fairly strong bonding in the complex ion $Fe(H_2O)_6{}^{3+}$.

Q4. What is the 'polarizing power' of a cation, and what factors tend to increase it?

A4. In Unit S4 (Bonding and Structure), you learned that the polarizing power of a cation is its ability to distort the charge cloud of a neighbouring anion, leading to partial covalent bonding. Polarizing power increases with increasing charge and with decreasing size.

Q5. Adjacent molecules can also be polarized by cations.

What might be the effect of polarization on the bonds in the $Fe(H_2O)_6{}^{3+}$ complex?

A5. The further distortion of the charge cloud in a water molecule, already polar due to the differing electronegativities of oxygen and hydrogen, leads to a strengthening of the Fe—O bonds by shifting electron density from the O—H bonds. The O—H bonds thus become weaker, and the release of protons becomes more likely.

Q6. Write an equation for the transfer of one proton from the hexaaqua-iron(III) ion to a water molecule.

A6. $Fe(H_2O)_6^{3+}(aq) + H_2O(l) \rightleftharpoons Fe(H_2O)_5OH^{2+}(aq) + H_3O^+(aq)$

This change is shown in diagram form below.

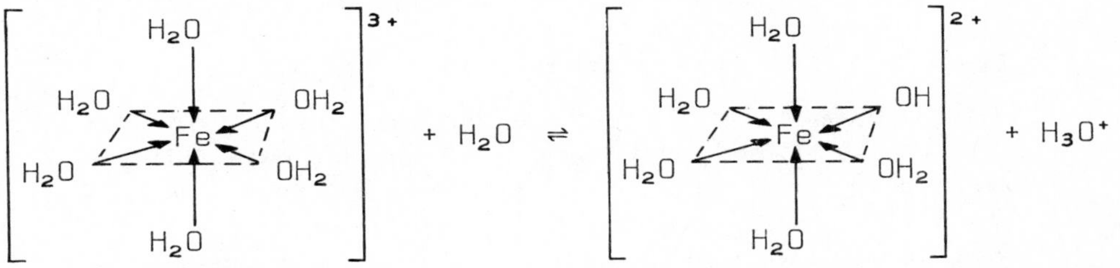

Q7. Why is the transfer of a second proton less likely to occur than the transfer of the first?

A7. The charge on Fe is effectively reduced from 3 to 2. The remaining H_2O ligands are thus less polarized and release protons less readily. However, a <u>small</u> amount of $Fe(H_2O)_4(OH)_2^+$ ion is formed.

Q8. In general terms, which transition metal ions would you expect to have the most strongly acidic aqua-complexes?

A8. The most strongly acidic aqua-complexes would be those formed from ions of small size and high charge. Elements in the first transition series have smaller ions of the same charge than the second and third transition series and, within a series, ions of the same charge become slightly smaller from left to right across the Periodic Table.

You can apply what you have learned to the following exercises.

Exercise 42 The compound VCl_4 dissolves in water with a violent reaction. Explain why the resulting solution is strongly acidic and contains oxovanadium(IV) ions, VO^{2+}. Assume a coordination number of 6.

(Answer on page **90**)

Exercise 43 (a) Show how the manganate(VII) ion, MnO_4^-, could be regarded as derived from interaction between the manganese(VII) ion, Mn^{7+}, and water molecules.

(b) The manganate(VII) ion could also be regarded as a complex ion formed from Mn^{7+} and O^{2-} ions. Suggest reasons why it is <u>not</u> usually regarded as a complex ion.

(Answers on page **91**)

The hydrolysis of aqua-complexes has some bearing on the variation of redox potentials with pH, as you see in the next section.

The effect of pH on redox potentials

You learned in Unit P6 (Equilibrium 3: Redox Reactions) how the redox potential of a half-cell varies from the standard value when the concentration of <u>any</u> species appearing in the half-equation varies from the standard 1.0 mol dm^{-3}. Use this knowledge to do the next exercise.

<u>Exercise 44</u> (a) Write a half-equation for the reduction of manganate(VII) to manganese(II) in acid solution.

(b) The standard redox potential for the half-cell in which this reaction occurs is 1.51 V. How would you expect the potential to change if the pH were adjusted to 1.0 without altering the other concentrations? (A qualitative answer only is expected, but you may wish to try to calculate a new value using the Nernst equation.)

(Answers on page **91**)

You may be surprised to learn that pH can also affect redox potentials in some cells where hydrogen ions do <u>not</u> appear in the half-equation. This arises when hydrolysis of one or more of the component ions occurs to produce an acidic solution, as we showed in the previous section.

For instance, the half-cell reaction normally written as:

$$Fe^{3+}(aq) + e^{-} \rightleftharpoons Fe^{2+}(aq)$$

does not represent <u>all</u> the changes which occur in the half-cell, because both $Fe^{3+}(aq)$ and $Fe^{2+}(aq)$ are hydrolysed to some extent. This means that other redox equilibria, such as

$$Fe(H_2O)_5OH^{2+}(aq) + e^{-} \rightleftharpoons Fe(H_2O)_5OH^{+}(aq)$$

also contribute to the electrode potential. The extent of their contribution varies with the pH of the solution, because changing $[H^+(aq)]$ alters the concentrations of the hydrolysed ions by shifting the position of equilibrium in acid-base reactions such as:

$$Fe(H_2O)_6{}^{3+}(aq) \rightleftharpoons Fe(H_2O)_5OH^{2+}(aq) + H^{+}(aq)$$

Therefore, the electrode potential for Fe^{3+}/Fe^{2+} does vary a little with pH, and the same is true for other systems where hydrolysis occurs. For this reason, electrode potentials for the transition metals are listed at zero pH. Under these conditions, the extent of hydrolysis is negligible.

Note that the stabilization by acid of Fe^{2+} solutions to oxidation by air is a <u>kinetic</u> effect and is not due to the dependence of electrode potential on pH.

You have seen how pH can affect electrode potentials and the relative stabilities of different oxidation states. Now we show how changing ligands can also affect the relative stabilities.

THE EFFECT ON REDOX CHEMISTRY OF CHANGING LIGANDS

We usually discuss the redox chemistry of the transition elements by reference to electrode potentials for the hydrated ions, i.e. complex ions with water molecules as ligands. When other ligands replace water molecules, the redox chemistry is modified and the relative stabilities of the different oxidation states may be changed.

Objective. When you have finished this section you should be able to:

(30) recognise that redox potentials for changes in oxidation state of transition elements vary according to the ligands present.

You should achieve this objective by doing the next exercise.

Exercise 45 Here are some redox potentials:

$Fe(CN)_6{}^{3-}(aq), Fe(CN)_6{}^{4-}(aq) \mid Pt;$ $E^\ominus = 0.36$ V

$I_2(aq), 2I^-(aq) \mid Pt;$ $E^\ominus = 0.54$ V

$Fe^{3+}(aq), Fe^{2+}(aq) \mid Pt;$ $E^\ominus = 0.77$ V

(a) What would you expect to observe when aqueous iodine is added to:

(i) $FeSO_4(aq)$, (ii) $K_4Fe(CN)_6(aq)$?

(b) What would you expect to observe when aqueous potassium iodide is added to:

(i) $FeCl_3(aq)$, (ii) $K_3Fe(CN)_6(aq)$?

(c) Summarise the information above in one sentence referring to the relative stabilities of Fe(II) and Fe(III).

(Answers on page 91)

The next section deals with the relative stabilities of copper(I) and copper(II) compounds. Again, the nature of the ligands is important.

SOME REDOX CHEMISTRY OF COPPER

As well as providing another example of the way ligands affect redox chemistry, this section also contains another application of solubility products and another example of disproportionation. You have met these two topics before - in Unit P2 (Equilibrium 1: Principles) and Unit I2 (The Halogens) respectively.

Objectives. When you have finished this section you should be able to:

(31) explain why copper(I) ions cannot exist in solution (except in minute concentration);

(32) describe and explain how some insoluble copper(I) compounds can be made.

Read about copper(I) compounds in your textbook. Look for methods of preparation and reasons why the only common ones are insoluble.

The first exercise in this section requires you to make predictions about the copper(I) oxidation state by using $E^\ominus$ values.

Exercise 46 $H_3PO_3(aq) + 2H^+(aq), H_3PO_2(aq) + H_2O(l) \mid Pt;$ $E^\ominus = -0.50$ V

$Cu^{2+}(aq), Cu^+(aq) \mid Pt;$ $E^\ominus = 0.15$ V

$Cu^+(aq) \mid Cu(s);$ $E^\ominus = 0.52$ V

(a) Use the $E^\ominus$ values above to explain why an attempt to reduce copper(II) to copper(I) in aqueous solution using dioxophosphoric(I) acid would probably not be successful.

(b) Copper(I) sulphate is reasonably stable as a dry solid but not in solution. What would you expect to happen if you dissolved it in water. What type of change is this?

(Answers on page **91**)

The next exercise concerns the relative stabilities of copper(I) and copper(II) in the presence of cyanide ions.

Exercise 47 In an excess of cyanide ions a copper(I) complex exists, $Cu(CN)_4{}^{3-}$, but there is no corresponding copper(II) complex. The relevant redox potentials are:

$Cu(CN)_4{}^{3-}(aq) + e^- \rightleftharpoons Cu(s) + 4CN^-(aq);$ $E^\ominus = -1.09$ V

$Cu^{2+}(aq) + 4CN^-(aq) + e^- \rightleftharpoons Cu(CN)_4{}^{3-}(aq);$ $E^\ominus = 1.77$ V

(a) What effect would the presence of cyanide ions have on the attempted reduction referred to in Exercise 46?

(b) Would copper metal be an effective reducing agent in these circumstances? Write an equation.

(Answers on page **91**)

You may well have used a reaction similar to the one referred to in Exercise 47(b) to prepare copper(I) chloride. The first step is to make a copper(I) complex, $CuCl_2{}^-$, by heating metallic copper and a copper(II) compound with an excess of chloride ions:

$$Cu(s) + Cu^{2+}(aq) + 4Cl^-(aq) \rightarrow 2CuCl_2{}^-(aq)$$

This complex is in equilibrium with a minute concentration of $Cu^+(aq)$, according to the equation:

$$CuCl_2{}^-(aq) \rightleftharpoons Cu^+(aq) + 2Cl^-(aq); \quad K_c = 5.0 \times 10^{-6} \text{ mol}^2 \text{ dm}^{-6}$$

When the solution is diluted, the equilibrium shifts to the right* and sufficient copper(I) ions are produced to cause precipitation of copper(I) chloride.

$$Cu^+(aq) + Cl^-(aq) \rightleftharpoons CuCl(s); \quad K_c = 3.1 \times 10^6 \text{ mol}^{-2} \text{ dm}^6$$

*It is easier to see why the equilibrium shifts to the right by applying Le Chatelier's principle to the equilibrium written in the form:

$$Cu(H_2O)_2Cl_2{}^-(aq) + 2H_2O(l) \rightleftharpoons Cu(H_2O)_4{}^+(aq) + 2Cl^-(aq)$$

In the next experiment you apply the principles we have just outlined to the practical preparation of copper(I) compounds.

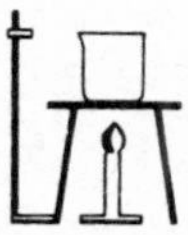

EXPERIMENT 5

Some redox chemistry of copper

Aim and Introduction

The purpose of this experiment is to prepare two copper(I) compounds by reduction of copper(II). Different conditions are used in Parts A, B and C.

Requirements

safety spectacles
boiling-tube and holder
spatula
copper turnings
copper(II) chloride-6-water, $CuCl_2 \cdot 6H_2O$
sodium chloride, NaCl
wash-bottle of distilled water
Bunsen burner and bench mat
beaker, 250 cm^3
4 test-tubes
test-tube rack
sodium sulphite-7-water, $Na_2SO_3 \cdot 7H_2O$
copper(II) sulphate solution, 0.10 M $CuSO_4$
potassium iodide solution, 0.10 M KI
sodium thiosulphate-5-water, $Na_2S_2O_3 \cdot 5H_2O$

Procedure - Part A

1. Put 1 spatula measure of copper turnings, two of copper(II) chloride and two of sodium chloride in a boiling-tube and add about 10 cm^3 of distilled water.

2. Heat the tube till the contents just boil, and maintain this temperature, swirling the tube from time to time, for several minutes until the solution appears not to be darkening in colour any further.

3. Allow the tube to cool a little, and pour the solution into about 50 cm^3 of distilled water in a beaker.

4. Put the beaker on one side while you do Part B of the experiment and then re-examine it.

Procedure - Part B

1. Dissolve one spatula measure of copper(II) chloride in water in a test-tube about one-third full.

Procedure - Part B (continued)

2. Dissolve one spatula measure of sodium sulphite in water in another test-tube about one-third full.
3. Mix the two solutions and allow to stand for a few minutes.
4. If necessary, pour off the solution to examine the white solid.

Questions - Parts A and B

1. What is the white solid produced in each case, and why has it no colour?
2. What is the reducing agent in each case?
3. Why was heat required in Part A and not in Part B?
4. What is the function of the excess of chloride ions in Part A?
5. What causes the dark brown colour in Part A?
6. Why does the solution in contact with the white solid in Part A slowly turn blue on standing?

(Answers on page 92)

Procedure - Part C

1. Mix a little copper(II) sulphate solution in a test-tube with about twice the volume of potassium iodide solution and allow to settle.
2. Explain the change in appearance after step 2.

Questions - Part C

1. What do you observe in step 1?
2. Explain the change in appearance after step 2.
3. Why is the solution no longer blue after step 2?
4. What, therefore, is the creamy white solid?

(Answers on page 92)

Summarise the whole experiment in a larger copy of Results Table 5.

Results Table 5

	Method	Observations	Equation(s)
A. Preparation of			
B. Preparation of			
C. Preparation of			

(Specimen results on page 92)

The reaction you performed in Part C of the experiment can be represented by the equation:

$$2Cu^{2+}(aq) + 4I^-(aq) \rightarrow 2CuI(s) + I_2(aq)$$

In the next exercise you consider this reaction as consisting of two half-reactions (redox) followed by precipitation.

$$Cu^{2+}(aq) + e^- \rightleftharpoons Cu^+(aq); \quad E^\ominus = 0.15\ V$$

$$I_2(aq) + 2e^- \rightleftharpoons 2I^-(aq); \quad E^\ominus = 0.54\ V$$

$$Cu^+(aq) + I^-(aq) \rightleftharpoons CuI(s); \quad K_c = 1/K_s = 1 \times 10^{12}\ mol^{-2}\ dm^6$$

Exercise 48 (a) Do the electrode potentials above lead you to expect iodide ions to reduce copper(II) to copper(I)? Explain.

(b) What is the maximum concentration of $Cu^+(aq)$ there can be in a suspension of copper(I) iodide where $[I^-(aq)] = 0.10$ mol dm^{-3}?

(c) The electrode potentials quoted above refer to standard conditions; in particular, $[Cu^+(aq)] = 1.0$ mol dm^{-3}. What is the effect on the electrode potential of reducing $[Cu^+(aq)]$ to the value calculated in (b)? (Either give a qualitative answer or, if you are familiar with the Nernst equation, calculate a new value.)

(d) In the light of your answer to (c), suggest a reason why the addition of iodide ions to copper(II) sulphate solution precipitates copper(I) iodide while the corresponding reaction with bromide ions does not occur.

$$2Br_2(aq) + 2e^- \rightleftharpoons 2Br^-(aq); \quad E^\ominus = 1.09 \text{ V}$$

(Assume CuBr has similar solubility to CuI.)

(Answers on page **92**)

We now move on to an important application of the redox chemistry of the transition metals - their use as catalysts, which we touched on in Level 1.

TRANSITION ELEMENTS IN CATALYSIS

In Unit P5 (Chemical Kinetics), you learned the distinction between homogeneous and heterogeneous catalysis. In this section we deal mainly with the mechanism of homogeneous catalysis; examples of heterogeneous catalysis appear in Unit I6 (Selected *p*-Block Elements).

Objectives. When you have finished this section you should be able to:

(33) explain a general mechanism for homogeneous catalysis involving transition metal ions, and give some examples;

(34) use standard redox potentials to predict whether particular ions might function as catalysts for a given reaction;

(34) describe very briefly the importance of transition metals in biological systems.

If it is available, watch the section on catalysis in the ILPAC video-programme 'Transition Metals' either now as an introduction, or at the end of this section as a summary.

Read the section in your textbook(s) dealing with homogeneous catalysis paying particular attention to the importance of transition elements.

You should now be able to do the following Revealing Exercise, which deals with the catalytic oxidation of 2,3-dihydroxybutanedioate (tartrate) ions by aqueous hydrogen peroxide. The exercise will help you to revise some aspects of redox chemistry you have studied earlier.

Q1. Write the formula for 2,3-dihydroxybutanedioate ion, both in structural and condensed forms.

A1. 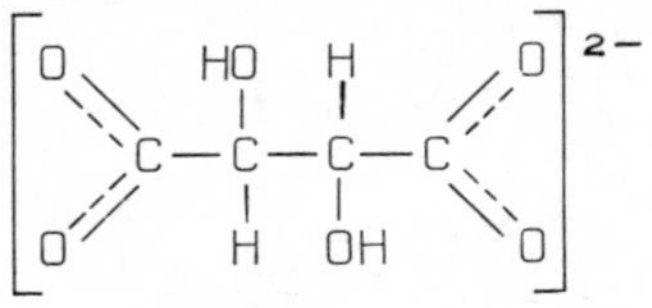

or

$CH(OH)CO_2^-$
|
$CH(OH)CO_2^-$

or $C_4H_4O_6^{2-}$

Q2. Deduce the half-equation for its oxidation to carbon dioxide and methanoate ion. In order to balance atoms <u>and</u> charges you need to include hydrogen ions and water.

A2. $C_4H_4O_6^{2-}(aq) + 2H_2O(l) \rightleftharpoons 2CO_2(g) + 2HCO_2^-(aq) + 6H^+(aq) + 6e^-$

Q3. Write a half-equation for the reduction of hydrogen peroxide to water.

A3. $H_2O_2(aq) + 2H^+(aq) + 2e^- \rightleftharpoons 2H_2O(l)$

Q4. The standard electrode potentials for half-cells in which these reactions occur are as follows:

$2HCO_2^-(aq) + 2CO_2(g) + 6H^+(aq) + 6e^- \rightleftharpoons C_4H_4O_6^{2-}(aq) + 2H_2O(l)$; $E^{\ominus} = 0.20$ V

$H_2O_2(aq) + 2H^+(aq) + 2e^- \rightleftharpoons 2H_2O(l)$; $E^{\ominus} = 1.77$ V

Do you think that hydrogen peroxide will oxidize 2,3-dihydroxybutanedioate ion?

A4. The reaction is energetically favourable. $\Delta E^{\ominus}$ is 1.57 V, which is large enough to suggest that the reaction would go to completion.

Q5. Write the overall equation for the reaction by combining the two half-equations.

A5. $C_4H_4O_6^{2-}(aq) + 3H_2O_2(aq) \rightarrow 2CO_2(g) + 2HCO_2^-(aq) + 4H_2O(l)$

Q6. Although it is energetically favourable, the reaction is very slow, even when heated, unless a catalyst is present. How, in general terms, does a catalyst speed up a reaction?

A6. A catalyst provides an alternative reaction pathway with lower activation energy.

Since this particular reaction involves a transfer of electrons, a catalyst could act in two possible ways.

Either: catalyst + H_2O_2 → intermediate
intermediate + $C_4H_6O_6{}^{2-}$ → products + catalyst

catalyst + $C_4H_6O_6{}^{2-}$ → intermediate
intermediate + H_2O_2 → products + catalyst

Q7. What type of reaction would be involved in <u>both</u> of these possibilities?

A7. Each would be a redox reaction.

Q8. What feature of transition elements makes their ions likely candidates for catalysts in redox reactions?

A8. Transition elements have more than one oxidation state. Electrons could, therefore, be transferred between reactants and products by means of the catalyst changing between two oxidation states.

The electron transfer can be represented generally as:

e^-

Reactant A + Catalyst (Low ox.) → Product A + Catalyst (High ox.)

e^-

Reactant B + Catalyst (High ox.) → Product B + Catalyst (Low ox.)

Overall: Reactant A + Reactant B → Product A + Product B

Q9. Cobalt(II) has been suggested as a suitable catalyst, with intermediate formation of cobalt(III). Assuming for the moment that simple ions $Co^{2+}(aq)$ and $Co^{3+}(aq)$ are involved, write equations for a possible mechanism. (Combine half-equations as before.)

A9. $H_2O_2(aq) + 2H^+(aq) + 2e^- \rightleftharpoons 2H_2O(l)$

$2Co^{2+}(aq) \rightleftharpoons 2Co^{3+}(aq) + 2e^-$

$H_2O_2(aq) + 2Co^{2+}(aq) + 2H^+(aq) \rightleftharpoons 2Co^{3+}(aq) + 2H_2O(l)$ ... (1)

$C_4H_4O_6{}^{2-}(aq) + 2H_2O(l) \rightleftharpoons 2CO_2 + 2HCO_2{}^-(aq) + 6H^+(aq) + 6e^-$

$6Co^{3+}(aq) + 6e^- \rightleftharpoons 6Co^{2+}(aq)$

$C_4H_4O_6{}^{2-}(aq) + 2H_2O(l) + 6Co^{3+}(aq) \rightleftharpoons 2CO_2(g) + 2HCO_2{}^-(aq)$
$+ 6H^+(aq) + 6Co^{2+}(aq)$ ... (2)

The combination of equations (1) and (2) gives the same overall reaction as before.

Q10. For this mechanism to be feasible, the standard electrode potential for the Co^{2+}/Co^{3+} half-cell must lie within a certain range of values. What range is this?

A10. $E^{\ominus}$ should lie between 0.2 V and 1.77 V so that Co(III) can oxidize 2,3-dihydroxybutanedioate ion and Co(II) can reduce hydrogen peroxide.

Q11. $E^{\ominus}$ for the half-cell $Co^{3+}(aq),Co^{2+}(aq) \mid Pt$ is 1.84 V, which is outside the required range. What two factors might, nevertheless, make Co(II) able to act as a catalyst for this reaction?

A11. (a) Using concentrations different from the standard concentrations implied by $E^{\ominus}$ values might make the reaction feasible. In particular, Co^{2+} in high concentration might reduce H_2O_2 in low concentration. However, concentration changes do not alter ΔE values very much.

(b) The cobalt ions can form complexes with the 2,3-dihydroxybutanedioate ions. Electrode potentials for half-cells involving complexes are often substantially different from those involving simple ions.

Unfortunately, $E^{\ominus}$ for the half-cell containing cobalt complexes with 2,3-dihydroxybutanedioate is not quoted in the literature. Even if it were, and the reaction were shown to be energetically favourable, we could still not be certain that Co(II) would be a catalyst because we have no means of predicting kinetic feasibility.

Clearly, you must do an experiment.

EXPERIMENT 6

Investigating the use of cobalt(II) ions as a catalyst

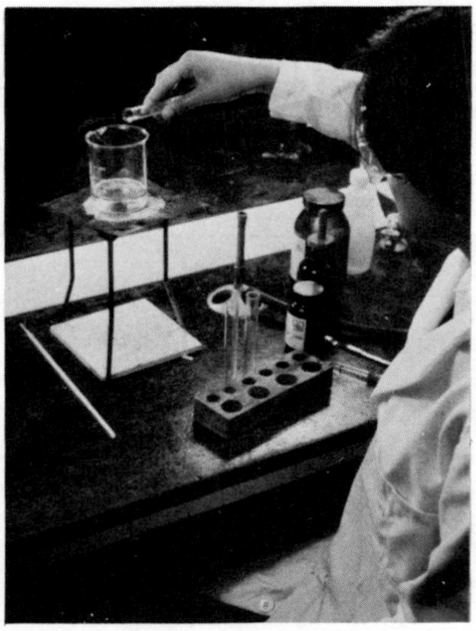

Aim

The purpose of this experiment is to test whether cobalt(II) ions will catalyse the reaction discussed in the last exercise (the oxidation of 2,3-dihydroxybutanedioate ions by hydrogen peroxide) and to look for evidence of intermediate compound formation.

Introduction

In this short experiment, you simply mix the hot reactants and add the potential catalyst. If you see a coloured intermediate, you can attempt to stabilize it by cooling the mixture quickly.

Requirements

safety spectacles
beaker, 250 cm^3
distilled water
spatula
potassium sodium 2,3-dihydroxybutanedioate, $CO_2K(CHOH)_2CO_2Na \cdot 4H_2O$
(also known as potassium sodium tartrate or Rochelle salt)
Bunsen burner and bench mat
tripod and gauze
thermometer, 0 - 100 °C
measuring cylinder, 25 cm^3
hydrogen peroxide solution, 20-volume H_2O_2 ---------------- 
2 test-tubes and rack
cobalt(II) chloride, $CoCl_2 \cdot 6H_2O$
stirring rod
teat pipette

Procedure

1. Dissolve about 1 g of potassium sodium 2,3-dihydroxybutanedioate in about 50 cm^3 water in a beaker.
2. Heat the solution to about 70 °C.
3. Add about 20 cm^3 hydrogen peroxide solution, heat again to about 70 °C and then remove from heat. At this stage there should be little or no sign of reaction.
4. Dissolve a few small crystals (about 0.25 g) of cobalt(II) chloride in a little water (about 5 cm^3) in a test-tube and add this to the hot solution. There will be an induction period before a reaction starts, so be patient! The length of the induction period decreases with increasing concentrations of reactants and catalyst and with increasing temperature. These can be varied if necessary.
5. As soon as the solution appears to be dark green, quickly transfer about 5-10 cm^3 by teat pipette to a test-tube and cool it under the tap. If the green colour has disappeared before you have cooled the tube, repeat the experiment in such a way that the reaction proceeds more slowly.

Questions

1. The gas given off when the reaction starts has two components. What are these?
2. What is the dark green solution and why does the colour return to pink?
3. Why does cooling the test-tube preserve the green colour for a while?

(Answers on page **92**)

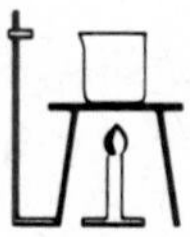

Another experiment (optional) on catalysis follows, but you have now covered enough ground to be able to do one or more of the following Teacher-marked Exercises, for which you have to make a broad review of all the characteristics of transition elements. Ask your teacher which question(s) to attempt.

Teacher-marked Exercise

A

The elements scandium to zinc are generally listed in a separate 'block' of the Periodic Table.

(a) Review the major characteristics common to this block of elements which are not generally shown by elements in other blocks of the Periodic Table. Explain how the chemical properties of these elements or their compounds can be understood in terms of electronic structure.

(b) Illustrate these characteristics by reference to ONE member of the series scandium to zinc, and discuss critically the extent to which this member exhibits all the characteristics outlined in your answer to (a).

Teacher-marked Exercise

A

Discuss, with appropriately chosen examples to illustrate your answers, some of the typical properties of the transition elements and their compounds.

Outline briefly THREE important applications of compounds of the transition elements.

Teacher-marked Exercise

A

(a) Show, by stating essential reagents and conditions only, how the following conversions may be brought about.

(i) $Mn^{2+}(aq) \rightarrow MnO_2(s)$

(ii) $MnO_2(s) \rightarrow MnO_4^{2-}(aq)$

(iii) $MnO_4^{2-}(aq) \rightarrow MnO_4^{-}(aq)$

(iv) $Mn^{2+}(aq) \rightarrow MnO_4^{-}(aq)$

(v) $Cr^{3+}(aq) \rightarrow CrO_4^{2-}(aq)$

(vi) $CrO_4^{2-}(aq) \rightarrow Cr_2O_7^{2-}(aq)$

(b) Sketch the structures of the ions CrO_4^{2-} and $Cr_2O_7^{2-}$.

(c) Both potassium manganate(VII) and potassium dichromate(VI) may be used as oxidizing agents in volumetric analysis. What are the advantages and disadvantages of each?

(d) A solution containing 0.124 g of arsenic(III) oxide (As_2O_3) required 25.0 cm^3 of acidified 0.02 M potassium manganate(VII) for complete oxidation. What was the oxidation state of the arsenic after oxidation?

For the next experiment you should make predictions about possible catalysts in the same way as we did in the Revealing Exercise. Then you will test your predictions. To make the best use of your laboratory time, you should make the predictions beforehand.

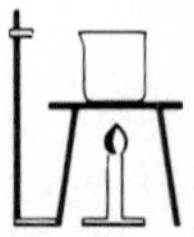

EXPERIMENT 7

Catalysing the reaction between iodide ions and peroxodisulphate ions

Aim

The purpose of this experiment is to find and test suitable catalysts, from a range of readily available transition metal ions, for the reaction:

$$S_2O_8^{2-}(aq) + 2I^-(aq) \rightarrow 2SO_4^{2-}(aq) + I_2(aq)$$

Introduction

You can make predictions about the suitability of possible catalysts by assuming that the mechanism of catalysis consists of two stages, either of which can be the first:

(i) higher oxidation state of catalyst oxidizes I^-,

(ii) lower oxidation state of catalyst reduces $S_2O_8^{2-}$.

You then perform a number of experiments, each with fixed starting concentrations of I^-, $S_2O_8^{2-}$ and possible catalyst. Thiosulphate ions and starch are also added to enable you to measure the rate of reaction, and thus test your predictions.

As the reaction proceeds, any iodine formed immediately reacts with the thiosulphate:

$$I_2(aq) + 2S_2O_3^{2-}(aq) \rightarrow S_4O_6^{2-}(aq) + 2I^-(aq)$$

When all the thiosulphate has reacted, the free iodine gives a deep blue colour with the starch. If t is the time taken for the blue colour to appear, then $1/t$ is a measure of the initial rate of reaction - see Unit P5 (Chemical Kinetics).

Requirements

safety spectacles
4 test-tubes and rack
potassium iodide solution, 0.2 M KI
sulphuric acid, dilute, 1 M H_2SO_4
potassium manganate(VII) solution, 0.1 M $KMnO_4$
potassium chromate(VI) solution, 0.1 M K_2CrO_4
iron(III) chloride solution, 0.1 M $FeCl_3$
potassium peroxodisulphate solution 0.2 M $K_2S_2O_8$
manganese(II) sulphate solution, 0.1 M $MnSO_4$
chromium(III) chloride solution, 0.1 M $CrCl_3$
iron(II) sulphate solution, 0.1 M $FeSO_4$
4 burettes and stands } (shared with other students)
4 beakers, 100 cm^3 } (shared with other students)
4 small funnels } (shared with other students)
starch solution, 0.2%
sodium thiosulphate solution, 0.01 M $Na_2S_2O_3$
conical flask, 150 cm^3
boiling-tube
stopclock

Procedure

1. In a copy of Results Table 6 write the appropriate electrode potentials from your data book.

2. Use the electrode potentials to predict the feasibility of each step in the proposed mechanism. You should wait till these steps have been tested before predicting the overall feasibility.

Results Table 6

Transition element		Chromium	Manganese	Iron
Oxidation states used		Cr(VI) Cr(III)	Mn(VII) Mn(II)	Fe(III) Fe(II)
Electrode potential/V (higher ox. state ⇌ lower)				
Electrode potential/V ($I_2 + 2e^- \rightleftharpoons 2I^-$)				
Electrode potential/V ($S_2O_8^{2-} + 2e^- \rightleftharpoons 2SO_4^{2-}$)				
Does higher ox. state oxidize I^-?	Prediction			
	Practically			
Does lower state reduce $S_2O_8^{2-}$?	Prediction			
	Practically			
Do you expect catalysis?				
Time for blue colour to appear/*s*				

(Specimen results on page 92)

3. In a test-tube, mix a few drops of potassium iodide solution with a few drops of dilute sulphuric acid. Add a few drops of one of the solutions containing a transition element in a higher oxidation state. Look for evidence of reaction and fill in your table accordingly.

4. In a test-tube, mix a few drops of potassium peroxodisulphate solution with a few drops of a solution containing the same transition element in a lower oxidation state. Look for evidence of reaction and fill in your table accordingly.

5. Repeat steps 3 and 4 for the other two transition elements. From your results predict which of the given solutions are likely to be catalysts.

   To check whether catalysis actually occurs, proceed as follows. (If you do not have time to check every prediction, share your results with other students.)

6. Fill 4 burettes with one each of the following solutions:

   potassium iodide, potassium peroxodisulphate,

   starch, sodium thiosulphate.

7. From the burettes run into a conical flask these volumes:

   10 cm^3 of potassium iodide solution,

   10 cm^3 of sodium thiosulphate solution,

   5 cm^3 of starch solution

8. Run 20 cm^3 of potassium peroxodisulphate solution into a boiling-tube.

9. Quickly pour the contents of the boiling-tube into the flask and start the stopclock. Swirl the flask twice to mix the contents and then stand it on the bench while you look for the appearance of a blue colour.

10. As soon as the solution turns blue, stop the clock and record the time taken.

11. Repeat steps 7 to 10, but in addition to the first three reagents, add 5 drops of a solution containing a transition metal ion.

12. If you have time to repeat the procedure before trying another possible catalyst then, of course, your results should be more reliable.

Questions

1. For one of the three transition elements you used, all of the predictions were confirmed by experiment. Which one was this? Describe briefly a possible mechanism (without equations) for catalysis involving this element.

2. One of the three transition elements did not catalyse the reaction. Which one was this? Why could it not function as a catalyst?

3. One of the three transition elements worked well as a catalyst, even though its lower oxidation state did not appear to react with peroxodisulphate. Which one was this? Suggest a possible explanation. (Hint: look at Experiment 2.)

4. Two students performed this experiment on different days using the same equipment and solutions. They found that their results did not agree very well. Suggest an explanation.

(Answers on page 93)

The experiments you have just done, together with the preceding exercise, illustrate the type of mechanism which is believed to operate in many examples of homogeneous catalysis. We now consider, very briefly, heterogeneous catalysis.

Heterogeneous catalysis

Transition elements and their compounds are widely used in industry as solid catalysts in gas phase reactions - you have already met a number of examples. Where the catalyst is a compound, e.g. vanadium(V) oxide in the manufacture of sulphuric acid, the mechanism probably involves electron transfer between two oxidation states in a manner similar to the homogeneous catalysis already described. This may also be the case when the catalyst is a metal initially but is converted to a compound by one of the reactants.

However, the mechanism of heterogeneous catalysis often involves a process known as chemisorption. Reacting gases are fairly strongly but reversibly bonded to the surface atoms of a transition metal, using the *d* orbitals. In the process some of the bonds within the gas molecules become stretched or even broken. In addition, the concentration of gases near the surface is increased. Both these factors increase the rate of reaction.

We do not discuss in detail any mechanisms for heterogeneous catalysis but you can find accounts in your textbooks if you wish to read about them. Ask your teacher if your syllabus includes this topic.

Catalysis is also important in biological systems, and this is mentioned briefly in the final section of this Unit.

Transition elements in biological systems

Although this aspect of transition element chemistry is rarely examined at A-level, your study would be incomplete without considering the great importance of transition elements in biological systems.

Ask your teacher for some references for reading on this topic if you cannot find much in your textbooks. Some items you may wish to pursue are as follows:

Anaemia and the role of iron in haemoglobin.

Cobalt in vitamin B12.

Transition elements as coenzymes (i.e. substances which enable enzymes to function as catalysts).

Diseases associated with deficiencies of copper, zinc and manganese.

Trace elements in soil.

LEVEL TWO CHECKLIST

You have now reached the end of this Unit. In addition to what was listed at the end of Level One, you should now be able to:

(20) & (21) use the equilibrium law to write expressions for stability constants of complex ions and to use them in simple calculations;

(22) explain the terms polydentate and chelate;

(23) explain why polydentate ligands generally give very stable complex ions;

(24) explain the use of complexes in titrimetric analysis;

(25) & (26) describe the shapes commonly adopted by complex ions and discuss examples of structural, geometric and optical isomerism;

(27) describe how the formula of a complex ion can be determined by colorimetry;

(28) explain why solutions of some complex ions are acidic;

(29) recognise that pH often affects redox potentials;

(30) recognise that redox potentials for changes in oxidation state of transition elements vary according to the ligands present;

(31) explain why copper(I) ions cannot exist in solution (except in minute concentration);

(32) describe and explain how some insoluble copper(I) compounds can be made;

(33) explain a general mechanism for homogeneous catalysis involving ions of transition elements, and give some examples;

(34) use standard redox potentials to predict whether particular ions might function as catalysts for a given reaction;

(35) describe very briefly the importance of transition metals in biological systems.

Check that you have adequate notes before going on to the End-of-Unit Test.

There is also an End-of-Unit Practical Test, which appears overleaf. Ask your teacher whether you should do this test as well.

END-OF-UNIT TEST

To find out how well you have learned the material in this Unit, try the test which follows. Read the notes below before starting.

1. You should spend about $1\frac{1}{2}$ hours on this test.

2. Hand your answers to your teacher for marking.

END-OF-UNIT PRACTICAL TEST

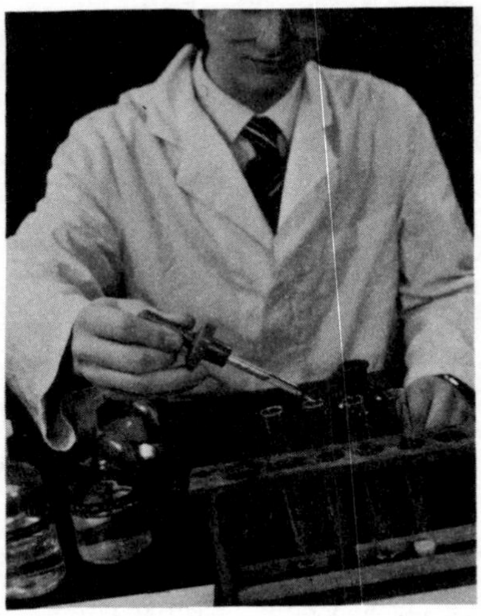

A part

This test is intended primarily for students preparing for a practical examination. Ideally, it should be done under examination conditions. We do not include a requirements list here because we assume that all the materials you need will be provided for you.

Ask your teacher whether you may refer to textbooks and/or notes during the test.

You are provided with two salts C and D. Carry out the following tests and record your observations and inferences in (a larger copy of) the table provided. Then answer the questions which follow the table.

Results Table 7

Test	Observations	Inferences
1. Warm three-quarters of your sample of C with 4-5 cm^3 of aqueous sodium hydroxide.		
2. Add approximately 10 cm^3 of dilute sulphuric acid to the remainder of your sample of C in a boiling-tube and warm the mixture in order to dissolve the solid. Use portions of the solution for the following tests: (a) To 1-2 cm^3 of the solution of C add an equal volume of aqueous potassium iodide. Then add, dropwise, aqueous sodium thiosulphate until there is no further change. (b) To 2 cm^3 of the solution add a little copper powder and warm. (c) To 3-4 cm^3 of the solution add a little zinc powder and allow the mixture to stand. It is suggested that you make observations for about 5 minutes and then allow the mixture to stand for a further 30 minutes, making observations from time to time. During this time you should proceed with other tests.		
3. Carry out a flame test on substance D.		
4. Dissolve some D in the minimum quantity of distilled water and use portions of the solution for the following tests: (a) Add a few drops of this solution to a mixture of 1-2 cm^3 of aqueous potassium iodide with an equal volume of dilute sulphuric acid. Then add aqueous sodium thiosulphate dropwise. (b) To 1 cm^3 of the solution of D add aqueous sodium hydroxide. Then add dilute sulphuric acid until in excess. (c) To about 2 cm^3 of the solution of D add an equal volume of dilute sulphuric acid. Then add hydrogen peroxide solution dropwise until there is no further change. (d) Transfer the solution from (c) to a boiling-tube and add about 10 cm^3 of aqueous sodium hydroxide and 1 cm^3 of hydrogen peroxide solution. Heat the resulting solution.		

The anion in D contains oxygen and a metal. Give the oxidation states of the metal which are indicated in the reactions in 4(a), 4(b) and 4(d).

END-OF-UNIT TEST

Questions 1-4 concern the following metals from the first *d*-block series in the Periodic Table:

A Scandium (atomic number 21)

B Titanium (atomic number 22)

C Manganese (atomic number 25)

D Iron (atomic number 26)

E Copper (atomic number 29)

A

Select, from A to E, the metal which

1. has the greatest number of unpaired electrons in its atom (1)

2. forms a colourless ion of oxidation state +4 (1)

3. forms the smallest cation of oxidation state +2 (1)

4. displays the highest oxidation number (1)

5. Titanium has the electronic structure $1s^2 2s^2 2p^6 3s^2 3p^6 3d^2 4s^2$ Which of the following suggested compounds of titanium is UNLIKELY to exist?

   A K_3TiF_6 C $K_2Ti_2O_5$ E $Ti(H_2O)_6Cl_3$

   B K_2TiF_6 D K_2TiO_4 (1)

6. A compound *X* has the formula $Cr(H_2O)_6Cl_3$ and a relative formula mass of 266. 20.0 cm^3 of a solution containing 13.30 g dm^{-3} of *X* required 10.0 cm^3 of 0.1 M $AgNO_3$ for complete precipitation of the chloride ions.

   A

   Which of the following is the best structural formula for *X*?

   A $Cr(H_2O)_6{}^{3+}3Cl^-$

   B $CrCl(H_2O)_5{}^{2+}2Cl^- \cdot H_2O$

   C $CrCl_2(H_2O)_4{}^+Cl^- \cdot 2H_2O$

   D $CrCl_3(H_2O)_3 \cdot 3H_2O$

   E $CrCl_3 \cdot 6H_2O$ (1)

In Questions 7 to 10 inclusive one, or more than one, of the suggested answers may be correct. You should answer as follows:

A

A if only 1, 2 and 3 are correct

B if only 1 and 3 are correct

C if only 2 and 4 are correct

D if only 4 is correct

E if some other response, or combination, is correct

7. In which of the following reactions is the named element oxidized?

1. Thallium in $2Tl^{+}(aq) + Zn(s) \rightarrow 2Tl(s) + Zn^{2+}(aq)$
2. Silver in $Ag_2S(s) + 4CN^{-}(aq) \rightarrow 2[Ag(CN)_2]^{-}(aq) + S^{2-}(aq)$
3. Copper in $2Cu^{2+}(aq) + 4I^{-}(aq) \rightarrow 2CuI(s) + I_2(aq)$
4. Gold in $4Au(s) + 8CN^{-}(aq) + 2H_2O(l) + O_2(g) \rightarrow 4[Au(CN)_2]^{-}(aq) + 4OH^{-}(aq)$ (1)

8. In which of the following ions does the metal have an oxidation number of +3?

1. VO^{2+} 2. AlO_2^{-} 3. $[Fe(CN)_6]^{4-}$ 4. $[CrCl_2(H_2O)_4]^{+}$ (1)

9. Which of the following compounds contain manganese in its highest oxidation state?

1. Mn_2O_7 2. MnC_2O_4 3. $KMnO_4$ 4. K_2MnO_4 (1)

10. Chromium forms the complex ion $[Cr(NH_3)_6]^{3+}$. Which of the following statements would you expect to be true?

1. The correct name is the hexammine-chromium(III) ion.
2. The complex ion is colourless.
3. The complex ion is octahedral.
4. A solution of the ions gives an immediate precipitate of chromium(III) hydroxide on addition of cold aqueous sodium hydroxide. (1)

For Questions 11 and 12, choose an answer from A to E as follows:

A

A Both statements true: second explains first.
B Both statements true: second does not explain first.
C First true: second false.
D First false: second true.
E Both false.

	First statement	Second statement	
11.	In $Co(NH_3)_6Cl_3$, the oxidation number of cobalt is +6.	The oxidation numbers of the constituents of a compound must add algebraically to zero.	(1)
12.	Chromium (atomic number 24) has a maximum oxidation number of VI.	Chromium has six electrons in its highest energy level.	(1)

13. (a) Explain the meaning of 'complex ion', as applied to transition metals, incorporating the terms 'ligand' and 'central ion' in your answer. (3)

A

(b) Complete the equations:

$M(H_2O)_4{}^{2+}(aq) + 4NH_3(aq) \rightarrow$
$M(H_2O)_4{}^{2+}(aq) + 4Cl^-(aq) \rightarrow$ (2)

(c) Suggest two possible shapes for the two different complex ions formed in reaction (b) (2)

(d) Name the TYPE of bonding common to both these complex ions in (c). (1)

(e) Say why ammonia molecules and chloride ions are able to form these complexes. (2)

(f) Explain, using an example, why the electronic configurations of transition metal ions are particularly appropriate for the formation of complex ions. (2)

(g) Write the formula of:

(i) the hexacyanoferrate(II) ion;

(ii) the hexacyanoferrate(III) ion. (2)

(h) Explain why chlorine can interconvert the complexes in (g) and write an equation for the reaction. (3)

(i) Suggest the observations that could be recorded if sulphur(IV) oxide (sulphur dioxide) gas is bubbled into a hot, acidified solution containing $Cr_2O_7{}^{2-}$ ions and say what type of reaction is involved. (3)

14. (a) In aqueous solution, the colours of certain vanadium ions are as follows:

A

$VO_2{}^+$ [i.e. V(V)], yellow; V^{4+}, blue; V^{3+}, green

When sulphur dioxide is passed through an acidic solution of ammonium vanadate (NH_4VO_3), the solution turns green. How would you find out experimentally whether the green colour was due to V^{3+}, or to a mixture of vanadium in oxidation states IV and V? (4)

(b) The reaction between peroxodisulphate ions, $S_2O_8{}^{2-}$, and iodide ions is catalysed by some transition metal ions. Describe how you would compare the catalytic effect of Cr^{3+} and Fe^{3+} ions on this reaction. (7)

(c) In fact, Fe^{3+} is found to be a catalyst, but not Cr^{3+}. Suggest a possible mechanism, in view of the following standard electrode potentials:

$Fe^{3+}(aq)$, $Fe^{2+}(aq)$	+0.77 V
$S_2O_8{}^{2-}(aq)$, $2SO_4{}^{2-}(aq)$	+2.01 V
$I_2(aq)$, $2I^-(aq)$	+0.54 V

What prediction can be made about the standard electrode potential of $Cr^{3+}(aq)$, $Cr^{2+}(aq)$ ions in view of the observation that Cr^{3+} ions do not catalyse the reaction? (6)

15. Consider the following standard electrode potentials, all of which refer to aqueous solutions.

A

$Cr^{3+}, Cr^{2+} \mid Pt$ $\quad E^{\ominus} = -0.41$ V

$(Cr_2O_7^{2-} + 14H^+), (2Cr^{3+} + 7H_2O) \mid Pt$ $\quad E^{\ominus} = +1.33$ V

$Ce^{4+}, Ce^{3+} \mid Pt$ $\quad E^{\ominus} = +1.70$ V

(a) Write down the equations for the half-cell reactions corresponding to these three standard electrode potentials. (3)

(b) Find the e.m.f. of the following cells, all concentrations being unity.

$Pt \mid Cr^{2+}, Cr^{3+} \,\vdots\, Ce^{4+}, Ce^{3+} \mid Pt$

$Pt \mid (2Cr^{3+} + 7H_2O), (Cr_2O_7^{2-} + 14H^+) \,\vdots\, Ce^{4+}, Ce^{3+} \mid Pt$ (3)

(c) In view of the e.m.f.'s so calculated, what would be expected to happen when a solution containing an equal number of moles of Ce^{3+} and Ce^{4+} ions was added to an acidified solution of Cr^{3+} ions? Write the equation for the reaction. (3)

16. (a) (i) How would you obtain an aqueous solution of the complex ion $[Cr(NH_3)_6]^{3+}$?

A

(ii) What is the oxidation state of chromium in this ion?

(iii) Give the stereo-structure of the ion.

(iv) Give the name of the ion, $[Cr(NH_3)_4Cl_2]^+$, and draw the stereo-structures of two isomers of it. (10)

(b) (i) Write an expression for the stability constant of the tetramminecopper(II) ion, $[Cu(NH_3)_4]^{2+}$.

(ii) When aqueous sodium hydroxide is added to a solution of this complex in water, a small quantity of copper(II) hydroxide is formed, but when hydrogen sulphide gas is passed through such a solution almost all the copper is precipitated as copper(II) sulphide. Suggest an explanation for this difference in behaviour. (7)

(Total 75 marks)

APPENDIX ONE

ELLINGHAM DIAGRAMS AND THE EXTRACTION OF METALS

This section is primarily for students following syllabuses which include the interpretation of Ellingham diagrams. If your teacher recommends that you study this topic, you should already have some knowledge of standard free energy change $\Delta G^{\ominus}$, and its relationship with enthalpy of reaction, entropy and temperature:

$$\Delta G^{\ominus} = \Delta H^{\ominus} - T\Delta S^{\ominus}$$

Before you begin, you may need to revise the work you did at the end of Unit S3 (Chemical Energetics). Alternatively, your teacher may have decided that you study that section now for the first time.

<u>Objectives</u>. When you have finished this section you should be able to:

(36) state the information conveyed by a single line on an <u>Ellingham diagram</u>;

(37) construct a simple <u>Ellingham diagram</u> from given thermodynamic data;

(38) interpret <u>Ellingham diagrams</u> so as to predict the feasibility of the <u>reduction of metal oxides by</u> carbon and carbon monoxide.

Read about Ellingham diagrams in your textbook(s) and their use in deciding the best method of extraction of metals. You should then be able to do the following exercises.

<u>Exercise 49</u> (a) What information is represented by a single line on an Ellingham diagram?

(b) For many chemical reactions $\Delta H^{\ominus}$ and $\Delta S^{\ominus}$ vary so little with temperature that they may be taken as effectively constant. This enables us to calculate values of $\Delta G^{\ominus}$ over a range of temperatures.

Reaction	$\Delta H^{\ominus}$(298 K) /kJ mol^{-1}	$\Delta S^{\ominus}$(298 K) /J mol^{-1} K^{-1}
2C(graphite) + O_2(g) → 2CO	-221	+180
2Fe(s) + O_2(g) → 2FeO(s)	-533	-151

Calculate $\Delta G^{\ominus}$ for each reaction at the following temperatures:

(i) 298 K (iii) 1500 K (v) 1808 K

(ii) 1000 K (iv) 1693 K (vi) 2000 K

(c) Using one pair of axes, plot an Ellingham diagram for the two reactions. Join adjacent points by straight lines, i.e. assume that intermediate values fall on the lines.

Exercise 49 (continued).

(d) Why do you think 'kinks' appear in the Fe $\rightarrow$ FeO line? (Hint: look up the melting-points of Fe and FeO.)

(e) Why does the C $\rightarrow$ CO line have a negative slope and the Fe $\rightarrow$ FeO line have a positive slope?

(Answers on page 93)

In the Revealing Exercise which follows you explore the use of Ellingham diagrams to give information about the best method of extraction of metals.

Metallic oxides may be reduced by heating with carbon provided that a temperature at which $\Delta G^\ominus$ for the reaction is negative can be achieved. We shall represent this reduction by the general equation:

$2MO(s) + 2C(s) \rightarrow 2M(s) + 2CO(g)$ - - - - - - - - - - (A)

Equation (A) can be thought of as a combination of two reactions:

$2C(s) + O_2(g) \rightarrow 2CO(g)$ - - - - - - - - - - - - - - -(B)

$2M(s) + O_2(g) \rightarrow 2MO(s)$ - - - - - - - - - - - - - - -(C)

Q1. How would you combine equations (B) and (C) to obtain equation (A)?

A1. If equation (C) is reversed (see equation (D) below) and added to equation (B), equation (A) is obtained.

$2MO(s) \rightarrow 2M(s) + O_2(g)$ - - - - - - - - - - - - (D)

$2C(s) + O_2(g) \rightarrow 2CO(g)$

$2C(s) + 2MO(s) + O_2(g) \rightarrow 2M(s) + 2CO(g) + O_2(g)$

Q2. If $\Delta G^\ominus$ for reaction (B) is $-x$ kJ mol^{-1}, and $\Delta G^\ominus$ for reaction (C) is $-y$ kJ mol^{-1}, what is the value of $\Delta G^\ominus$ for reaction (A)?

A2. $\Delta G^\ominus$ for reaction (A) = $\Delta G^\ominus$ for reaction (B) $-\Delta G^\ominus$ for reaction (C).

$= -x - (-y)$ kJ mol^{-1} = $(-x + y)$ kJ mol^{-1}

Study the Ellingham diagram below. Note that the temperatures are given in °C.

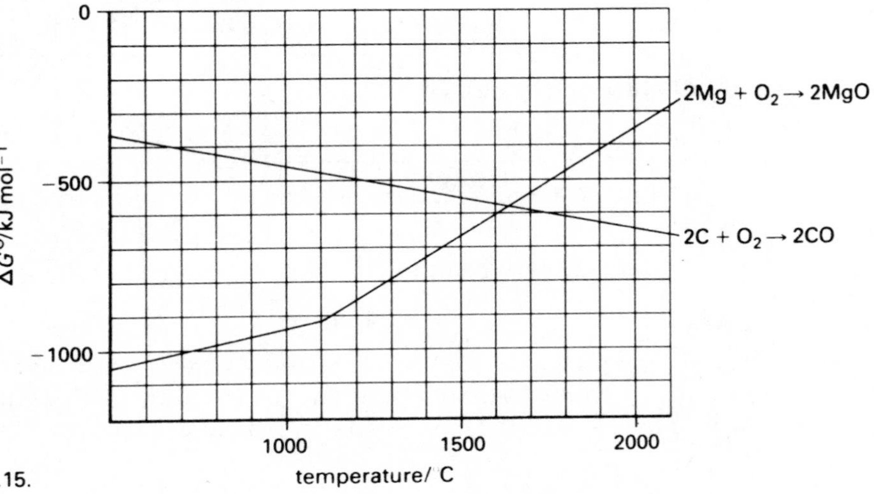

Fig.15.

Q3. What are the values of $\Delta G^{\ominus}$ for the reactions:

$2C(s) + O_2(g) \rightarrow 2CO(g)$

$2Mg(s) + O_2(s) \rightarrow 2MgO(s)$

at 1630 °C (the point of intersection)?

A3. $2C(s) + O_2(g) \rightarrow 2CO(g)$; $\Delta G^{\ominus} = -570\ \text{kJ mol}^{-1}$

$2Mg(s) + O_2(g) \rightarrow 2MgO(s)$; $\Delta G^{\ominus} = -570\ \text{kJ mol}^{-1}$

Q4. What is the value of $\Delta G^{\ominus}$ at 1630 °C for the following reaction?

$2MgO(s) + 2C(s) \rightarrow 2Mg(s) + 2CO(g)$

Show your working.

A4. $\Delta G^{\ominus} = -570\ \text{kJ mol}^{-1} - (-570\ \text{kJ mol}^{-1}) = 0$ (See A2.)

Q5. Use the Ellingham diagram to obtain values of $\Delta G^{\ominus}$ for the same reaction at 1000 °C and 2000 °C.

A5. At 1000 °C, $\Delta G^{\ominus} = -460\ \text{kJ mol}^{-1} -(-940\ \text{kJ mol}^{-1}) = +480\ \text{kJ mol}^{-1}$

At 2000 °C, $\Delta G^{\ominus} = -650\ \text{kJ mol}^{-1} -(-340\ \text{kJ mol}^{-1}) = -310\ \text{kJ mol}^{-1}$

Q6. Is the reduction of MgO by C feasible at 1000 °C and 2000 °C? Explain.

A6. The reduction of MgO by C at 1000 °C is not feasible because $\Delta G^{\ominus}$ is large and positive but at 2000 °C it is feasible because $\Delta G^{\ominus}$ is large and negative.

Q7. What is the significance of the point of intersection of the two lines?

A7. The point of intersection gives the minimum temperature at which the reaction is feasible since that is the temperature at which $\Delta G^{\ominus} = 0$.

Strictly, the reaction proceeds to an equilibrium mixture if $\Delta G^{\ominus}$ lies between ± 30 kJ mol^{-1} but we can ignore this here since it represents only a very small temperature range - see Unit S3 (Chemical Energetics).

Now attempt the next exercise, which is about the reduction of iron oxide. It helps to explain the operation of the blast furnace, which we describe in the section beginning on page 26 of this Unit, and uses a diagram similar to the one you drew in Exercise 49.

Exercise 50 Iron ore contains either iron(III) oxide, Fe_2O_3, or iron(II) diiron(III) oxide, Fe_3O_4. These are readily reduced to iron(II) oxide, FeO, by carbon or carbon monoxide. The key step in the process is the final reduction of iron(II) oxide, FeO.

Study the Ellingham diagram in Fig. 16 and answer the questions which follow.

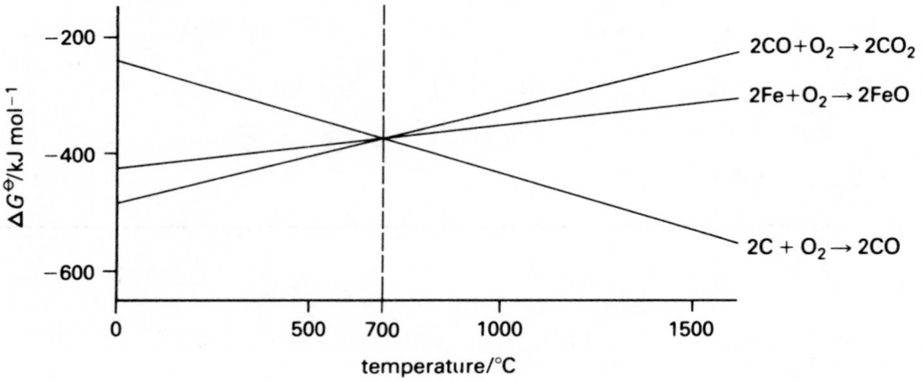

Fig.16. Ellingham diagram for the reduction of iron oxide.

Over what temperature ranges might iron(II) oxide be reduced by

(a) carbon, (b) carbon monoxide?

Explain your answers.

(Answers on page 93)

To consolidate your understanding of Ellingham diagrams, try the following exercise, in which you consider the feasibility of reducing metal oxides by various means. You will need to study Fig. 17.

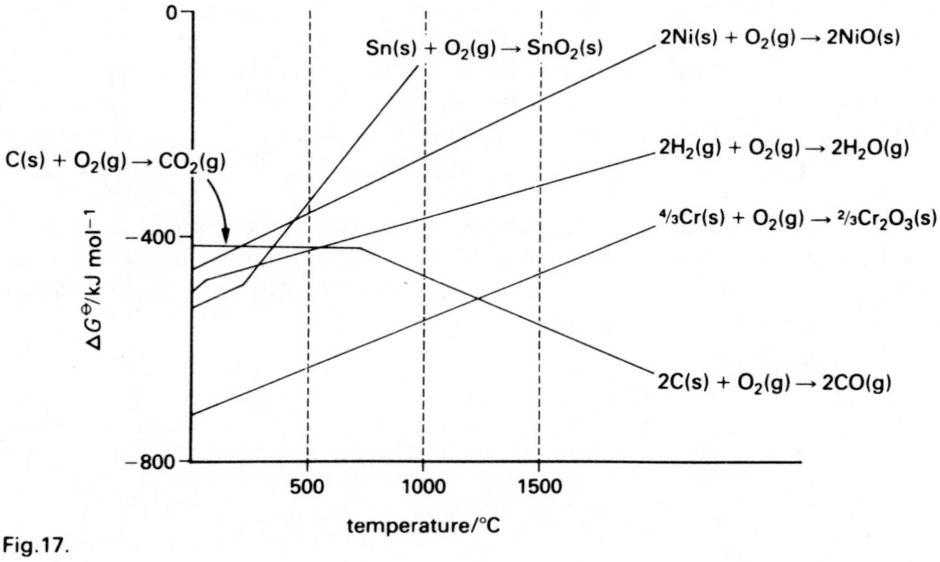

Fig.17.

Exercise 51 From the Ellingham diagram above, it can be deduced that

A

(a) carbon can reduce chromium(III) oxide at 1000 °C

(b) nickel(II) oxide can be reduced by hydrogen at 1500 °C

(c) below 300 °C nickel could reduce tin(IV) oxide

(d) both hydrogen and carbon could reduce tin(IV) oxide at 500 °C

(Answer on page 93)

Finally in this Appendix, we suggest that you try one or both of the following Teacher-marked Exercises. You may need to do some additional reading to help you plan your answer(s) before you start writing.

✓

Teacher-marked Exercise Fig. 18 shows the variation of the standard free energy change with temperature for the reaction of certain elements with oxygen according to the equations shown.

A

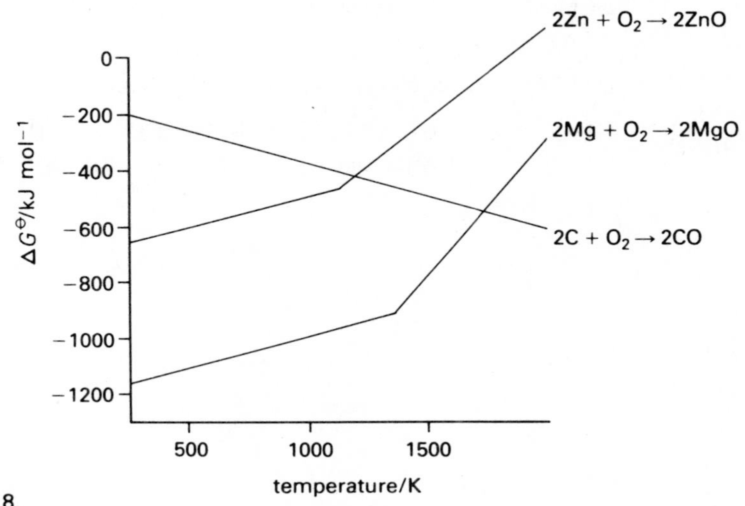

Fig.18.

(a) The standard enthalpy changes for all these reactions hardly vary with temperature. Explain qualitatively why the standard free energy change for the reaction $2C + O_2 \rightarrow 2CO$ decreases with a rise in temperature, whereas for metals, the standard free energy change for the reaction $2M + O_2 \rightarrow 2MO$ increases with a rise in temperature.

(b) Explain carefully how and why the information presented in Fig. 18 enables the feasibility to be assessed of the reduction of zinc oxide to zinc by (i) carbon at 800 K, (ii) magnesium at 1000 K and (iii) carbon at 1500 K.

(c) Use Fig. 18 to comment on the thermal stability of magnesium oxide, with respect to decomposition into magnesium and oxygen, at 1500 K.

(d) Why is it that several metals are prepared by electrolytic methods?

Teacher-marked Exercise

A

For the reaction: $Ti(s) + O_2(g) \rightarrow TiO_2(s)$

the free energy changes at various temperatures are given in the following table:

Temperature/K	300	600	1200	2000
ΔG/kJ mol^{-1}	-856	-801	-276	-330

and for the reaction, $2C(s) + O_2(g) \rightarrow 2CO(g)$

the free energy changes at various temperatures are given in the following table:

Temperature/K	300	600	1200	2000
ΔG/kJ mol^{-1}	-276	-330	-440	-582

(a) For the two sets of data, plot ΔG/kJ mol^{-1} (on the Y axis) against temperature/K (on the X axis), using the same axes.

(b) What information do the graphs provide about the feasibility of producing titanium by the reduction of titanium(IV) oxide by carbon?

(c) Suggest the possible difficulties which prevent such a method being used for the commercial production of titanium.

(d) Outline how titanium is produced from its chloride.

(e) Give a use of titanium and state a characteristic property of the element upon which its use depends.

APPENDIX TWO

In this Appendix we pick up two of the topics mentioned earlier in the Unit and take them a little further. This is because some of the accounts usually given at A-level (and expected in examinations) are rather inadequate, as you may already have realised.

Objectives. When you have finished the section you should be able to:

(39) give a simple account of the colour of transition metal compounds in terms of the ligand field theory;

(40) explain the variation in paramagnetism between different complex ions.

We begin with an elementary description of the ligand field theory to account for the colours of transition metal compounds.

Ligand field theory

In Level One we briefly explained the existence of highly-coloured compounds by stating that transition elements have electronic energy levels sufficiently close for the absorption of visible light by the promotion of electrons from one level to another. We did not say which levels are involved because the situation is not as simple as it might appear.

Although the $3d$ and $4s$ levels are very much closer in transition metal ions than are, say, the $2p$ and $3s$ levels in a sodium ion, the gap is usually still too large for visible light to cause electron transitions.

The ligand field theory explains how the presence of ligands cause the $3d$-orbitals, normally at the same energy level, to split into two levels with a gap suitable for the absorption of visible light. The reason is that the spatial arrangement of the d-orbitals (five of them, remember) is not the same as that of the ligands. Orbitals closer to the ligands are raised to a slightly higher energy level than those further away.

For more details, look up ligand field theory or crystal field theory in an advanced text. Some A-level texts may deal with the subject in an elementary way, without using these titles, in sections dealing with the colours of complex ions.

The distribution of electrons in the doubly-degenerate d-orbitals not only explains the colours of complex ions, but is also significant in other topics such as paramagnetism, as you see in the next section.

Paramagnetism

We noted in Level One that paramagnetism in transition element chemistry is associated with unpaired electrons. The way electrons are paired in simple ions is adequate to explain the variation in paramagnetism (the measured quantity is known as paramagnetic susceptibility) of hydrated ions also, as shown in Table 7.

Table 7

Ion	3*d* electrons	Unpaired electrons	Paramagnetism (relative)
Sc^{3+}	[ ] [ ] [ ] [ ] [ ]	0	0
Ti^{3+}	[↑] [ ] [ ] [ ] [ ]	1	1
V^{3+}	[↑] [↑] [ ] [ ] [ ]	2	2
Cr^{3+}	[↑] [↑] [↑] [ ] [ ]	3	3
Mn^{2+}	[↑] [↑] [↑] [↑] [↑]	5	5
Fe^{3+}	[↑] [↑] [↑] [↑] [↑]	5	5
Fe^{2+}	[↑↓] [↑] [↑] [↑] [↑]	4	4
Co^{2+}	[↑↓] [↑↓] [↑] [↑] [↑]	3	3
Ni^{2+}	[↑↓] [↑↓] [↑↓] [↑] [↑]	2	2
Cu^{2+}	[↑↓] [↑↓] [↑↓] [↑↓] [↑]	1	1
Zn^{2+}	[↑↓] [↑↓] [↑↓] [↑↓] [↑↓]	0	0

The numbers of unpaired electrons shown in Table 7 do not, however, explain the relative paramagnetism of all complexes. For instance, while $Fe(H_2O)_6{}^{2+}$ is strongly paramagnetic due to the same four unpaired electrons as in Fe^{2+}, the apparently similar complex ion $Fe(CN)_6{}^{4-}$ is not paramagnetic at all!

Ligand field theory explains this too. The splitting of the *d* energy levels varies in extent from ligand to ligand. If the energy gap is great enough, electrons may pair up in the lower sub-level, leaving the upper sub-level empty.

For further discussion of paramagnetism, read the appropriate section of your textbook or reference book.

Also, look again at the section on magnetism in the ILPAC video-programme 'The Transition Metals', if it is available.

ANSWERS

(Answers to questions from examination papers are provided by ILPAC and not by the Examination Boards.)

Exercise 1

(a)

Scandium	$1s^2 2s^2 2p^6 3s^2 3p^6 3d^1 4s^2$
Titanium	[Ar] $3d^2 4s^2$
Vanadium	[Ar] $3d^3 4s^2$
Chromium	[Ar] $3d^5 4s^1$
Manganese	[Ar] $3d^5 4s^2$
Iron	[Ar] $3d^6 4s^2$
Cobalt	[Ar] $3d^7 4s^2$
Nickel	[Ar] $3d^8 4s^2$
Copper	[Ar] $3d^{10} 4s^1$
Zinc	[Ar] $3d^{10} 4s^2$

(You might not have predicted $4s^1$ for chromium and copper using the simple rules; we explore this in Exercise 2.)

(b)

		3*d*					4*s*
Scandium	[Ar] :	↑					↑↓
Titanium	[Ar] :	↑	↑				↑↓
Vanadium	[Ar] :	↑	↑	↑			↑↓
Chromium	[Ar] :	↑	↑	↑	↑	↑	↑
Manganese	[Ar] :	↑	↑	↑	↑	↑	↑↓
Iron	[Ar] :	↑↓	↑	↑	↑	↑	↑↓
Cobalt	[Ar] :	↑↓	↑↓	↑	↑	↑	↑↓
Nickel	[Ar] :	↑↓	↑↓	↑↓	↑	↑	↑↓
Copper	[Ar] :	↑↓	↑↓	↑↓	↑↓	↑	↑
Zinc	[Ar] :	↑↓	↑↓	↑↓	↑↓	↑↓	↑↓

Note that electrons in the same energy level remain unpaired if possible. This is energetically more favourable because paired electrons repel each other more than unpaired electrons; we discussed this in Unit S2 (Atomic Structure).

Exercise 2

(a) For chromium, the $3d^5 4s^1$ configuration is at a lower energy level than $3d^4 4s^2$ because the former has more unpaired electrons. The extra repulsion between paired electrons, as compared to unpaired electrons, outweighs the small energy difference between the 3*d* and 4*s* levels.

For copper, the $3d^{10} 4s^1$ configuration is more stable than $3d^9 4s^2$ for the same reason.

Note that the so-called 'extra stability of the half-filled sub-shell' is a description of this effect and not an explanation.

(b) Molybdenum: $1s^2 2s^2 2p^6 3s^2 3p^6 3d^{10} 4s^2 4p^6 4d^5 5s^1$

Silver: $1s^2 2s^2 2p^6 3s^2 3p^6 3d^{10} 4s^2 4p^6 4d^{10} 5s^1$

Again, the repulsion between two paired 5*s* electrons outweighs the small energy difference between the 4*d* and 5*s* levels.

Exercise 3

Stable electron arrangements might be expected from loss of:

(a) all 3*d* and 4*s* electrons giving a noble gas configuration,

(b) the 4*s* electrons only, leaving the 3*d* untouched,

(c) the 4*s* and some 3*d* electrons leaving the 3*d* sub-shell half-filled.

Note that as the number of electrons lost increases, the stability of the resulting ions usually decreases. However, you see higher oxidation states in covalent structures.

Exercise 4

			3*d*				
(a)	Sc^{3+}	[Ar] :					
(b)	Ti^{2+}	[Ar] :	↑	↑			
(d)	V^{2+}	[Ar] :	↑	↑	↑		
(f)	Cr^{+}	[Ar] :	↑	↑	↑	↑	↑
(h)	Mn^{2+}	[Ar] :	↑	↑	↑	↑	↑
(i)	Fe^{2+}	[Ar] :	↑↓	↑	↑	↑	↑
(j)	Fe^{3+}	[Ar] :	↑	↑	↑	↑	↑
(k)	Co^{2+}	[Ar] :	↑↓	↑↓	↑	↑	↑
(m)	Ni^{2+}	[Ar] :	↑↓	↑↓	↑↓	↑	↑
(n)	Cu^{+}	[Ar] :	↑↓	↑↓	↑↓	↑↓	↑↓
(p)	Zn^{2+}	[Ar]	↑↓	↑↓	↑↓	↑↓	↑↓

			3*d*				
(c)	Ti^{3+}	[Ar] :	↑				
(e)	V^{3+}	[Ar]	↑	↑			
(g)	Cr^{3+}	[Ar]	↑	↑	↑		
(l)	Co^{3+}	[Ar]	↑↓	↑	↑	↑	↑
(o)	Cu^{2+}	[Ar]	↑↓	↑↓	↑↓	↑↓	↑↓

Note that the configurations in the first column all conform to the criteria listed in Exercise 3. Some of the ions listed are not very stable in aqueous solution, but do exist, e.g. Ti^{2+}, Cr^{+}.

Exercise 5

(a) $Ox(\text{Mn}) + 4Ox(\text{O}) = \text{charge}$

$\therefore\ Ox(\text{Mn}) = -1 - 4(-2) = -1 + 8 = +7$

The other answers are obtained similarly:

(b) +4 (d) +6 (f) +3 (h) +5 (j) +5

(c) +6 (e) +6 (g) +6 (i) +4 (k) +5

Exercise 6

(a) From Sc to Mn, the maximum oxidation state commonly occurs. This involves loss (or partial loss) of all 4*s* and 3*d* electrons giving a noble gas structure.

(b) From Mn to Zn, an oxidation state involving only the loss of 4*s* electrons commonly occurs.

Experiment 1. Specimen results

Table 2

Ion (hydrated)	VO_2^+	VO^{2+}	V^{3+}	V^{2+}
Colour	Yellow	Blue	Green	Violet
Oxidation state	5	4	3	2
Name	Dioxovanadium(V)	Oxovanadium(IV)	Vanadium(III)	Vanadium(II)

Results Table 1

Test	Observations	Summary of reaction(s)
Ammonium vanadate + acid	The white solid turned red and dissolved to a yellow solution.	$\overset{+5}{VO_3^-} \rightarrow \overset{+5}{VO_2^+}$
Vanadium(V) + zinc	The zinc effervesced and the yellow solution became green, blue, green again and, eventually, violet.	$\overset{+5}{VO_2^+} \rightarrow \overset{+4}{VO^{2+}} \rightarrow V^{3+} \rightarrow V^{2+}$
Vanadium(II) + manganate(VII)	The violet solution became green, blue, green, yellow and, finally, pink.	$V^{2+} \rightarrow V^{3+} \rightarrow VO^{2+} \rightarrow VO_2^+$
Vanadium(V) + sulphite. Add vanadium(II)	The yellow solution became blue. On adding V(II) the mixture became green.	$\overset{+5}{VO_2^+} \rightarrow \overset{+4}{VO^{2+}}$ $\overset{+4}{VO^{2+}} + V^{2+} \rightarrow V^{3+}$
Vanadium(V) + iodide + thiosulphate	The yellow solution became a muddy brown. Addition of thiosulphate gave a clear blue solution.	$\overset{+5}{VO_2^+} \rightarrow \overset{+4}{VO^{2+}}$
Vanadium(II) + concentrated sulphuric acid	The violet solution became green.	$V^{2+} \rightarrow V^{3+}$

Experiment 1. Questions

1. The first appearance of a green colour is due to a mixture of yellow vanadium(V) and blue vanadium(IV).
2. The subsequent changes are due to continuing reduction.

   Blue → green : V(IV) → V(III)

   Green → violet : V(III) → V(II) (slow)

   These changes are reversed on adding manganate(VII) except that when oxidation is complete the solution is pink.

Experiment 1. Questions (cont.)

3. The addition of iodide ions turned the solution a muddy brown. Iodine was produced in the reaction.
4. Sodium thiosulphate was added to remove iodine and reveal the blue colour of vanadium(IV).
5. Since the zinc half-cell has the most negative electrode potential of those shown, it can perform all the reduction stages. But the electrode potentials show that iodide will reduce V(V) to V(IV) but not V(IV) to V(III):

   $$2VO_2^+(aq) + 4H^+(aq) + 2I^-(aq) \rightleftharpoons 2VO^{2+}(aq) + 2H_2O(l) + I_2(aq)$$

   $$\Delta E^\ominus = 1.00\ V - 0.54\ V = +0.46\ V$$

   A positive value for $\Delta E^\ominus$ shows the reaction is feasible (from left to right as written).

   $$2VO^{2+}(aq) + 4H^+(aq) + 2I^-(aq) \rightleftharpoons 2V^{3+}(aq) + 2H_2O(l) + I_2(aq)$$

   $$\Delta E^\ominus = 0.34\ V - 0.54\ V = -0.20\ V$$

   A negative value for $\Delta E^\ominus$ shows that this reaction is not feasible under standard conditions.
6. The addition of sulphite ions (which combine with acid to give H_2SO_3)* readily reduces V(V) to V(IV) giving a blue solution, but does not cause further reduction to V(III) despite the prediction from electrode potentials:

   $$2VO^{2+}(aq) + 4H^+(aq) + H_2SO_3(aq) + H_2O(l) \rightleftharpoons$$
   $$2V^{3+}(aq) + 2H_2O(l) + SO_4^{2-}(aq) + 4H^+(aq)$$

   which, on cancelling $H^+(aq)$ and $H_2O(l)$, gives:

   $$2VO^{2+}(aq) + H_2SO_3(aq) \rightleftharpoons 2V^{3+}(aq) + H_2O(l) + SO_4^{2-}(aq)$$

   $$\Delta E^\ominus = 0.34\ V - 0.17\ V = +0.17\ V$$

   Note that a greenish colour may appear if excess sulphite is added, but this is due to the alternative oxidation product $S_2O_6^{2-}$ which decomposes in acid solution to give sulphur. Filtering the greenish mixture gives a blue solution.
7. To oxidize V(II) to V(III) but not V(III) to V(IV) we need a mild oxidizing agent with an electrode potential between -0.26 V and +0.34 V. Sulphuric acid (appearing in the table as $SO_4^{2-} + 4H^+$) with $E^\ominus$ = 0.17 V should be suitable, and you can confirm that the careful addition of a few drops of concentrated sulphuric acid to a solution of V(II) does produce green V(III).

   $$2V^{2+}(aq) + SO_4^{2-}(aq) + 4H^+(aq) \rightleftharpoons 2V^{3+}(aq) + H_2SO_3(aq) + H_2O(l)$$

   $$\Delta E^\ominus = 0.17\ V - (-0.26\ V) = +0.43\ V$$

   This helps to explain why the final stage in the reduction with zinc is rather slow. A fairly high concentration of sulphuric acid is needed in the first place to dissolve the ammonium trioxovanadate(V), but the final reduction of V(III) to V(II) will not occur until the zinc has lowered the concentration of acid somewhat by forming hydrogen.

*Equations may show $H_2SO_3(aq)$, $2H^+(aq) + SO_3^{2-}(aq)$, or $SO_2(aq) + H_2O(l)$. See Unit I6 (Selected *p*-Block Elements).

Exercise 7

For acid conditions, combining the first two equations gives:

$MnO_2(s) + 4H^+(aq) + Mn^{2+}(aq) \rightleftharpoons 2Mn^{3+}(aq) + 2H_2O(l)$; $\Delta E^\ominus = -0.56$ V

Since $\Delta E^\ominus$ is negative and fairly large, the reaction will not proceed from left to right to any measurable extent under standard conditions. Increasing $[H^+(aq)]$ still further would shift the equilibrium somewhat to the right, but not sufficiently to give an appreciable amount of $Mn^{3+}(aq)$, because $\Delta E^\ominus$ is outside the range of reversibility (i.e. -0.4 V to +0.4 V). For alkaline conditions, combining the last two equations gives:

$MnO_2(s) + 2H_2O(l) + Mn(OH)_2(s) + \cancel{OH^-(aq)} \rightleftharpoons 2Mn(OH)_3(s) + \cancel{OH^-(aq)}$;

$\Delta E^\ominus = +0.30$ V

Since $\Delta E^\ominus$ is positive, but less than 0.40 V, we should expect this reaction to proceed from left to right to an equilibrium mixture containing significant amounts of both reactants and products. However, since two of the reactants are solids, we might expect the reaction to be slow.

Since $OH^-(aq)$ does not appear in the final equation, changing its concentration will not change $\Delta E^\ominus$.

Exercise 8

Combining the two half-equations (multiplying the first by 5 to equalise the number of electrons) gives:

$5Mn^{2+}(aq) + MnO_4^-(aq) + 8H^+(aq) \rightleftharpoons Mn^{2+}(aq) + 4H_2O(l) + 5Mn^{3+}(aq)$;

which reduces to: $4Mn^{2+}(aq) + MnO_4^-(aq) + 8H^+(aq) \rightleftharpoons 4H_2O(l) + 5Mn^{3+}(aq)$

$\Delta E^\ominus = 1.50\text{ V} - 1.51\text{ V} = -0.01$ V

$\Delta E^\ominus$ is negative, which means that the reaction from left to right is not favoured under standard conditions, but it should be possible to make $\Delta E^\ominus$ appreciably positive by increasing the hydrogen ion concentration. This will shift the equilibrium to the right.

Exercise 9

For reaction in acid conditions, combining the first two half-equations gives:

$MnO_4^{2-}(aq) + 2H^+(aq) + MnO_2(s) + H_2O(l) \rightleftharpoons 2MnO_3^-(aq) + H_2O(l) + 2H^+(aq)$

which reduces to:

$MnO_4^{2-}(aq) + MnO_2(s) \rightleftharpoons 2MnO_3^-(aq)$; $\Delta E^\ominus = 2.0\text{ V} - 2.5\text{ V} = -0.5$ V

Since $\Delta E^\ominus$ is negative, the reaction from left to right is not favoured, and the equilibrium cannot be shifted to the right by changing $[H^+(aq)]$ since H^+ does not appear in the equation.

For the reaction in alkaline conditions, combining the third and fourth half-equations gives:

$MnO_4^{2-}(aq) + H_2O(l) + MnO_2(s) + 2OH^-(aq) \rightleftharpoons 2MnO_3^-(aq) + 2OH^-(aq) + H_2O(l)$

which reduces to:

$MnO_4^{2-}(aq) + MnO_2(s) \rightleftharpoons 2MnO_3^-(aq)$; $\Delta E^\ominus = 0.34\text{ V} - 0.84\text{ V} = -0.5$ V

The equation is identical with the first, and the conclusions are similar - the reaction from left to right is not favoured and equilibrium cannot be shifted to the right by changing $[OH^-(aq)]$.

Experiment 2. Questions

1. The worked example on page 13 led us to expect formation of Mn(VI) only in alkaline solution. (You may have noticed that the filter paper appears to act as a catalyst for this reaction.)
2. The addition of acid caused disproportionation of Mn(VI) to Mn(VII) (pink solution) and Mn(IV) (brown solid). The reduction in $[OH^-(aq)]$ caused the equilibrium to shift back to the left:

   $2MnO_4^-(aq) + MnO_2(s) + 4OH^-(aq) \rightleftharpoons 3MnO_4^{2-}(aq) + 2H_2O(l)$
3. Dilution of the Mn(III) solution caused disproportionation by shifting the equilibrium back to the left:

   $4Mn^{2+}(aq) + MnO_4^-(aq) + 8H^+(aq) \rightleftharpoons 4H_2O(l) + 5Mn^{3+}(aq)$
4. There is no red colouration.
5. The reactants are solids, which often react slowly.
6. The off-white precipitate of manganese(II) hydroxide darkens on standing, especially where it is in contact with the air. This fact suggests that manganese(II) hydroxide is readily oxidized to brown manganese(IV) oxide.

Exercise 10

(a) (i) Cr: $1s^2 2s^2 2p^6 3s^2 3p^6 3d^5 4s^1$

(ii) Cr^{2+}: $1s^2 2s^2 2p^6 3s^2 3p^6 3d^4$

(b) (i) +6 (ii) +6

(c) (i) Acid-base. The change is reversible according to the pH of the solution, and there is no change in oxidation state.

$Cr_2O_7^{2-}(aq) + H_2O(l) \rightleftharpoons 2CrO_4^{2-}(aq) + 2H^+(aq)$

(ii) Reduction. *Ox*(Cr) changes from +6 to +3.

(d) $Cr_2O_7^{2-}(aq) + 14H^+(aq) + 6e^- \rightleftharpoons 2Cr^{3+}(aq) + 7H_2O(l)$; $E^\ominus = +1.33$ V

Any reducing agent appearing on the right-hand side of a half-equation with a value of $E^\ominus$ less than 1.33 V should be able to effect the change. Bearing in mind that reactions involving solutions are generally faster than those involving solids, one might choose familiar reducing agents such as $Fe^{2+}(aq)$, $SO_2(aq)$, and $H_2S(aq)$, but there are many others listed.

Exercise 11

There are not very many. Lead iodide, PbI_2, which is bright yellow, is one you are likely to have seen. Others include dilead(II) lead(IV) oxide or 'red lead', Pb_3O_4, and the iodine chlorides, ICl (brown) and ICl_3 (yellow).

Exercise 12

Scandium ions, Sc^{3+}, have no electrons in the $3d$ or $4s$ orbitals. Therefore, electron transitions involving such electrons are not possible.

Zinc ions, Zn^{2+}, and copper(I) ions, Cu^+, have complete $3d$ sub-shells. The electron transitions responsible for the colour of transition elements always involve partly-filled orbitals. (Further discussion of these transitions is beyond A-level but is mentioned in Appendix Two.)

Exercise 13

	Central ion	Ligand(s)	Co-ordination number
(a)	Cu^{2+}	NH_3	4
(b)	Cr^{3+}	Cl^-, H_2O	6
(c)	Co^{2+}	OH^-, H_2O	6
(d)	V^{3+}	F^-	6

Exercise 14

(a) $Cu(H_2O)_4{}^{2+}$: tetraaquacopper(II)

(b) $Fe(CN)_6{}^{3-}$: hexacyanoferrate(III)

(c) $NiCl_4{}^{2-}$: tetrachloronickelate(II)

(d) $Ag(NH_3)_2{}^{+}$: diamminesilver(II)

Note that the suffix 'ate' is used only for anions.

Exercise 15

1. Ionic bonding between Cu^{2+} (or $Cu(H_2O)_4{}^{2+}$) and $SO_4{}^{2-}$.
2. Covalent bonding between S and O in $SO_4{}^{2-}$ ions and between H and O in H_2O molecules.
3. Dative covalent bonding between Cu^{2+} and H_2O (or co-ordinate bonding).
4. Hydrogen bonding between the fifth water molecule and the $SO_4{}^{2-}$ ion.

Exercise 16

Industrial reactions include:

1.	$N_2 + 3H_2 \rightleftharpoons 2NH_3$ (manufacture of ammonia)	Fe
2.	$2SO_2 + O_2 \rightleftharpoons 2SO_3$ (manufacture of sulphuric acid)	V_2O_5
3.	$4NH_3 + 5O_2 \rightleftharpoons 4NO + 6H_2O$ (manufacture of nitric acid)	Pt
4.	$2C_2H_4 + O_2 \rightleftharpoons 2C_2H_4O$ (manufacture of anti-freeze)	Ag
5.	$RR'C{=}CR''R''' + H_2 \rightleftharpoons RR'CHCHR''R'''$ (manufacture of margarine)	Ni

General reactions include:

1.	$Zn(s) + 2H^+(aq) \rightleftharpoons Zn^{2+}(aq) + H_2(g)$	Cu (introduced as Cu^{2+})
2.	$2H_2O_2 \rightleftharpoons 2H_2O + O_2$	MnO_2
3.	$2KClO_3 \rightleftharpoons 2KCl + 3O_2$	MnO_2
4.	$C_6H_6 + Br_2 \rightleftharpoons C_6H_5Br + HBr$	Fe (or $FeBr_3$)

Exercise 17

The density of scandium (3 g cm^{-3}) is much lower than the others (mostly 7-8 g cm^{-3}). The melting-point of zinc (420 °C) is much lower than the others (mostly above 1500 °C).

Their anomalous physical properties provide another reason (in addition to the absence of partly-filled *d*-orbitals in compounds) for excluding scandium and zinc from the transition metals.

Exercise 18

There is a general decrease in radii, both metallic and ionic, from Ti to Cu. This is because the additional electrons are accommodated in the same sub-shell, which is drawn closer to the nucleus by the higher nuclear charge.

There is a general, though irregular, increase in first ionization energy from Ti to Cu. The electron removed in ionization, though always removed from the same sub-shell, is progressively more tightly bound because it is only partially shielded from the increasing nuclear charge.

There is a general, though slightly irregular, increase in electronegativity from Ti to Cu. This parallels the decrease in atomic radius.

Exercise 19

Most data books do not list radii for ions of the same charge for all the elements in Period 1. In particular, the ionic radius of M^{2+} is listed only for Be. It is important when making comparisons to compare like with like.

Exercise 20

(a) The trends are in the same direction, i.e. radii decrease, while ionization energies and electronegativities increase.

(b) The range of the trends is very much greater for the short period elements than for the transition elements. For example, atomic radius varies from 0.124 nm (Fe) to 0.145 nm (Ti) in the transition elements, a difference of only 17%. In Period 1, atomic radius varies from 0.060 nm (O) to 0.152 nm (Li), a difference of 153%!

(c) In 'building-up' the elements in a short period, e.g. from sodium to chlorine, the extra electrons are all added to the outer shell. The outer electron shell is not very effectively shielded from the increasing nuclear charge and is therefore drawn closer and closer to the nucleus, giving a considerable decrease in atomic radius across the period until a noble gas is formed. (The mutual repulsion of four pairs of electrons in a noble gas structure results in an increase in radius.)

However, in 'building-up' the transition elements, the extra electrons are all added to an inner shell. The outer electrons which determine the radius of the atom are, therefore, more effectively shielded from the increased nuclear charge, so the decrease in radius is less marked than in a short period. [More details in Unit I3 (The Periodic Table).]

The trends in ionization energy and electronegativity are explained in the same way, since they depend largely on atomic radius. The closer an electron shell is to the nucleus, the more energy is required to remove an electron from it (the higher the ionization energy), and the more readily will other electrons be attracted in covalent bonding (the higher the electronegativity).

Exercise 21

(a) The densities of the transition elements are generally high (except for scandium - see Exercise 17). The densities of the *s*-block metals are generally low, especially in Group I. Note particularly that copper is about ten times as dense as potassium.

Densities of individual atoms increase markedly across a period because the atomic radii decrease (as explained in Exercise 20) while the atomic masses increase. Bulk densities increase similarly for the same packing arrangements. The difference in densities between transition metals and Group I metals is accentuated by the fact that most transition metals have close-packed structures while Group I metals do not.

(b) The melting-points of transition metals are generally high (above 1500 °C), except for zinc (see Exercise 17). The melting-points of *s*-block metals are generally low, especially in Group I.

Melting-point is an approximate indication of the strength of bonding between particles. Strong bonding occurs in the transition metals where the metallic radius is small and the structures are close-packed. In the *s*-block metals metallic bonding is weaker because the metallic radius is larger. The difference is again most marked when comparing transition metals with Group I metals, which have the largest metallic radii and do not have close-packed structures. In addition, they have only one valency electron per atom to contribute to the 'sea of electrons'. (You recall that metallic bonding may be simply pictured as attraction between metal ions and this 'sea of electrons'.)

(c) The boiling-points of transition metals are generally high (above 2000 °C), except for zinc again (see Exercise 17). The boiling-points of *s*-block metals are generally low, especially in Group I.

Boiling-point is also an approximate indication of the strength of bonding between particles. The explanations of similarities and differences are therefore the same as in part (b) above.

Note that boiling-point is a better indication of bonding strength than melting-point because vaporization separates the particles completely. Beware, however, of relating boiling-point to the strength of covalent bonding within molecules - when molecular substance vaporize, it is only the weak van der Waals bonds which are broken, and boiling-point is therefore only related to the strength of van der Waals bonding.

Note also that the question could have asked for a discussion of enthalpies of fusion and vaporization in parts (b) and (c). The answers would be almost identical.

Exercise 22

A. Brass is an alloy of copper and zinc.

B. Most coins are made from alloys containing copper and nickel (cupro-nickel).

C. Spanners are made from steel (iron) toughened by adding small quantities of metals such as chromium, vanadium and molybdenum.

D. Powerful permanent magnets are made from an alloy of aluminium, nickel and cobalt (Alnico).

E. Steel (iron) rails are made more resistant to wear by alloying with manganese.

F. Stainless steel is an alloy of iron, chromium and nickel.

Exercise 23

The similar atomic (and ionic) radii of the transition elements makes it possible for atoms (or ions) of one element to replace those of another element in the same solid structure. Thus, it is possible to make alloys containing transition elements in a wide range of composition.

However, because the radii are not identical, some deformation of the structure occurs and it is this which modifies the physical properties. (The way in which deformation of structure affects properties is beyond the scope of most A-level syllabuses.)

Exercise 24

(a) Copper (also gold, silver, and platinum).

(b) Silver (also gold and platinum).

(c) (i) $Mn(s) + 2H^+(aq) \rightarrow Mn^{2+}(aq) + H_2(g)$

(ii) $Ni(s) + 2H_2SO_4(l) \rightarrow NiSO_4(s) + 2H_2O(l) + SO_2(g)$

(Some $NiSO_4$ dissolves in the mixture of acid and water.)

(iii) $2Cr(s) + 3I_2(s) \rightarrow 2CrI_3(s)$ (v) $4V(s) + 5O_2(g) \rightarrow 2V_2O_5(s)$

(iv) $2Cr(s) + 6F_2(g) \rightarrow 2CrF_6(s)$ (vi) $Ti(s) + 2S(s) \rightarrow TiS_2(s)$

Exercise 25

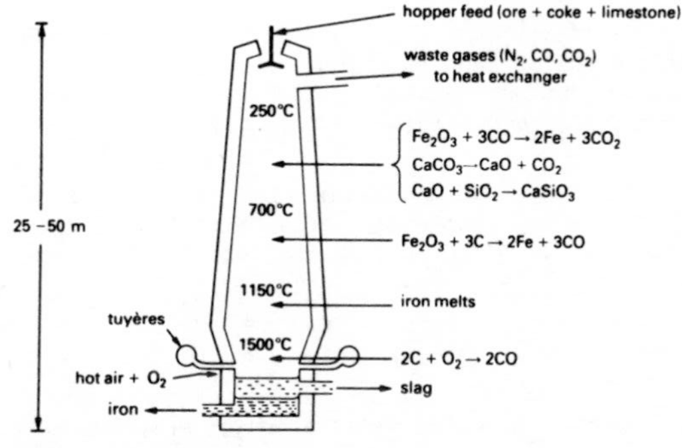

Fig.9. Extraction of iron in a blast furnace.

Exercise 26

(a) The chief impurities are carbon, silicon, phosphorus and sulphur.

(b) The impurities make cast iron harder and more brittle than pure iron.

(c) Cast iron is used to a limited extent for guttering, railings and fire-grates. High-grade cast iron is used for engine blocks.

Exercise 27

(a) (i) Iron(III) oxide, Fe_2O_3. Iron(II) diiron(III) oxide, Fe_3O_4.

(ii) Carbon and silicon, phosphorus or sulphur.

(b) (i) Limestone (calcium carbonate).

(ii) $CaCO_3(s) + SiO_2(s) \rightarrow CaSiO_3(l) + CO_2(g)$

(iii) Calcium silicate leaves as a liquid.

(c) (i) Carbon monoxide. $Fe_2O_3(s) + 3CO(g) \rightarrow 2Fe(s) + 3CO_2(g)$

or $Fe_3O_4(s) + 4CO(g) \rightarrow 3Fe(s) + 3CO_2(g)$

(ii) Carbon. $Fe_2O_3(s) + 3C(s) \rightarrow 2Fe(s) + 3CO(g)$

or $Fe_3O_4(s) + 4C(s) \rightarrow 3Fe(s) + 4CO(g)$

(d) (i) Carbon monoxide is the flammable gas.

(ii) The waste gas may be used directly in a heat exchanger to heat the air/oxygen blast and may be burned to provide heat to raise steam for running turbines.

(e)

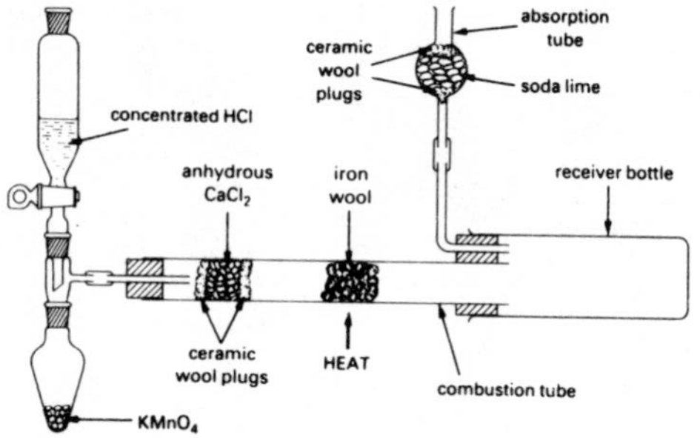

(Note that iron(III) chloride vapour at lower temperatures consists chiefly of Fe_2Cl_6 molecules, in which each iron atom is surrounded tetrahedrally by four chlorine atoms. The solid has a layer structure in which each iron atom is surrounded octahedrally by six chlorine atoms, each of which is attached to two iron atoms. The structures are very similar to those for aluminium chloride.)

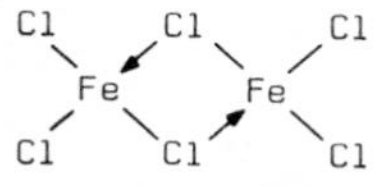

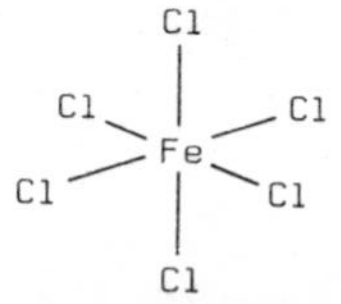

Exercise 28

(a) The oxygen oxidizes the impurities, especially carbon. Carbon monoxide is formed and this burns at the mouth of the converter.

(b) Oxygen is preferred because air contains nitrogen. The nitrogen not only is ineffective in removing carbon but also forms a small proportion of iron nitride which tends to make the steel brittle.

(c) The lining of a converter consists of silica, SiO_2, or calcined dolomite, $CaO + MgO$. Its function is to insulate the converter and, in the case of the dolomite, to assist in the removal of acidic oxides such as those of phosphorus and sulphur.

(d) The slag consists mostly of silicates of calcium and magnesium, with smaller proportions of sulphates and phosphates derived from the impurities in the iron. If the phosphorus content of the original iron ore is high enough, the slag may be used as a fertilizer.

(e) Steel with a moderate carbon content can be made very hard by rapid cooling (quenching) but it is also brittle. The strength may be increased greatly without losing too much hardness by carefully re-heating the quenched steel at a fixed temperature for a certain time. This process, known as 'tempering', alters the micro-structure of the steel and this results in improved properties.

Exercise 29

(a) Tetrachlorocuprate(II) ion.

(b) (i) $Cu(H_2O)_4{}^{2+}(aq) + Cl^-(aq) \rightleftharpoons Cu(H_2O)_3Cl^+(aq) + H_2O(l)$

$$K_1 = \frac{[Cu(H_2O)_3Cl^+]}{[Cu(H_2O)_4{}^{2+}]\,[Cl^-]}$$

(ii) $Cu(H_2O)_3Cl^+(aq) + Cl^-(aq) \rightleftharpoons Cu(H_2O)_2Cl_2(aq) + H_2O(l)$

$$K_2 = \frac{[Cu(H_2O)_2Cl_2]}{[Cu(H_2O)_3Cl^+]\,[Cl^-]}$$

(iii) $Cu(H_2O)_2Cl_2(aq) + Cl^-(aq) \rightleftharpoons Cu(H_2O)Cl_3{}^-(aq) + H_2O(l)$

$$K_3 = \frac{[Cu(H_2O)Cl_3{}^-]}{[Cu(H_2O)_2Cl_2]\,[Cl^-]}$$

(iv) $Cu(H_2O)Cl_3{}^-(aq) + Cl^-(aq) \rightleftharpoons CuCl_4{}^{2-}(aq) + H_2O(l)$

$$K_4 = \frac{[CuCl_4{}^{2-}]}{[Cu(H_2O)Cl_3{}^-]\,[Cl^-]}$$

(c) $K_1 \times K_2 \times K_3 \times K_4 =$

$$\frac{[Cu(H_2O)_3Cl^+][Cu(H_2O)_2Cl_2][Cu(H_2O)Cl_3{}^-][CuCl_4{}^{2-}]}{[Cu(H_2O)_4{}^{2+}][Cl^-][Cu(H_2O)_3Cl^+][Cl^-][Cu(H_2O)_2Cl_2][Cl^-][Cu(H_2O)Cl_3{}^-][Cl^-]}$$

$$= \frac{[CuCl_4{}^{2-}]}{[Cu(H_2O)_4{}^{2+}][Cl^-]^4}$$

(d) The unit for K is $\dfrac{\text{mol dm}^{-3}}{(\text{mol dm}^{-3})(\text{mol dm}^{-3})^4} = \text{mol}^{-4}\ \text{dm}^{12}$

Exercise 30

The relevant equation is:

$Ag(H_2O)_2^+(aq) + 2CN^-(aq) \rightleftharpoons Ag(CN)_2^-(aq) + 2H_2O(l)$

or $Ag^+(aq) + 2CN^-(aq) \rightleftharpoons Ag(CN)_2^-(aq)$

The stability constant for the complex ion is the equilibrium constant for this reaction.

$$K = \frac{[Ag(CN)_2^-(aq)]}{[Ag^+(aq)][CN^-(aq)]^2} = 1.0 \times 10^{21}\ mol^{-2}\ dm^6$$

Exercise 31

$$K = 1.0 \times 10^{21}\ mol^{-2}\ dm^6 = \frac{[Ag(CN)_2^-(aq)]}{[Ag^+(aq)][CN^-(aq)]^2}$$

$$\therefore [Ag^+(aq)] = \frac{[Ag(CN)_2^-(aq)]}{1.0 \times 10^{21}\ mol^{-2}\ dm^6 \times [CN^-(aq)]^2}$$

$$= \frac{0.10\ mol\ dm^{-3}}{1.0 \times 10^{21}\ mol^{-2}\ dm^6 \times (0.50)^2\ mol^2\ dm^{-6}}$$

$$= \frac{0.10\ mol\ dm^{-3}}{1.0 \times 10^{21} \times 2.5 \times 10^{-1}} = \boxed{4.0 \times 10^{-22}\ mol\ dm^{-3}}$$

Exercise 32

The ligand is called diaminoethane (formerly ethylenediamine). It would form two bonds with a central cation and is therefore bidentate. The molecule has two nitrogen atoms and these are the only ones with lone pairs of electrons available to make dative (or co-ordinate) bonds with a central cation.

Exercise 33

(a) The oxygen atoms and nitrogen atoms have lone pairs available to form dative bonds. However, there are ten of these (2 x N and 8 x O) in one ion of edta and only six bonds are formed. The only symmetrical way of forming six bonds is to use both nitrogen atoms and four of the eight oxygen atoms. Your model should show how the edta structure 'wraps round' the central ion in such a way that six bonds, and only six, can be directed towards the central ion.

(b) (i) The formation of dative bonds draws electrons away from the O—H bonds, encouraging the release of protons.

(ii) Only one of the two oxygen atoms in each carboxyl group can form bonds because of the way the edta molecule 'wraps around' the central ion. It is not possible to have both atoms close enough to the central ion to form bonds.

(c) The greater the number of bonds, the more difficult it will be to remove the ligand and, therefore, the more stable the complex ion. (This simple rule is not universally true because it assumes all dative bonds are of equivalent strength.)

Experiment 3. Specimen results

Results Table 3

Ligand	H_2O		Cl^-		$C_2O_4^{2-}$ = ox		$NH_2C_2H_4NH_2$ = en		$C_{10}H_{14}O_8N_2^{4-}$ = edta	
Complex ion	$Cu(H_2O)_4^{2+}$		$CuCl_4^{2-}$		$Cu(ox)_2^{2-}$		$Cu(en)_2^{2+}$		$Cu(edta)^{2-}$	
Colour	Blue		Yellowish-green		Blue		Violet		Light-blue	
Stability constant	-		4.0×10^5 $mol^4\ dm^{-12}$		2.1×10^{10} $mol^2\ dm^{-6}$		-		6.3×10^{18} $mol\ dm^{-3}$	
	Predictions (P) and results (R). ✓ = replacement, x = none									
	P	R	P	R	P	R	P	R	P	R
Add H_2O			x	✓	x	x		x	x	x
Add Cl^-	✓	✓			x	x		x	x	x
Add ox	✓	✓	✓	✓				x	x	x
Add en	✓	✓	✓	✓	✓	✓			x	x
Add edta	✓	✓	✓	✓	✓	✓		✓		

Experiment 3. Questions

1. Yes. Generally, polydentate ligands give more stable complexes than monodentate ligands, stability increasing with the number of bonds formed. This is only a general rule, however, and it is possible to have a complex containing, say, strongly bonded monodentate ligands which is more stable than one containing weakly bonded bidentate ligands.

2. Since *en* ligands displace *ox* ligands, but not vice versa, and they are both bidentate, $Cu(en)_2^{2+}$ must have a substantially greater stability constant than $Cu(ox)_2^{2-}$. It is not directly comparable with the stability constant for $Cu(edta)^{2-}$ which has different units because edta is hexadentate.

3. H_2O and Cl^- ligands appear to be readily interchangeable when concentrations are changed.

4. $Cu^{2+}(aq) + 4Cl^-(aq) \rightleftharpoons CuCl_4^-(aq)$

$$K_{st} = \frac{[CuCl_4^{2-}(aq)]}{[Cu^{2+}(aq)][Cl^-(aq)]^4} = 4.0 \times 10^5\ mol^{-4}\ dm^{-12}$$

$$\therefore \frac{[CuCl_4^{2-}(aq)]}{[Cu^{2+}(aq)]} = 4.0 \times 10^5\ mol^{-4}\ dm^{-12} \times [Cl^-(aq)]^4$$

(a) $\frac{[CuCl_4^{2-}(aq)]}{[Cu^{2+}(aq)]} = 4.0 \times 10^5 \times 5.0^4 = \boxed{2.5 \times 10^8}$

(b) $\frac{[CuCl_4^{2-}(aq)]}{[Cu^{2+}(aq)]} = 4.0 \times 10^5 \times 0.05^4 = \boxed{2.5}$

These figures show that dilution of the solution will soon reduce $[Cl^-(aq)]$ sufficiently to convert a significant proportion of $CuCl_4^{2-}$ ions to $Cu(H_2O)_4^{2+}$ ions and so change the colour.

Exercise 34

(a) $Cu(H_2O)_4^{2+}(aq) + 4NH_3(aq) \rightleftharpoons Cu(NH_3)_4^{2+}(aq) + 4H_2O(l)$

or $Cu^{2+}(aq) + 4NH_3(aq) \rightleftharpoons Cu(NH_3)_4^{2+}(aq)$

$Cu(H_2O)_4^{2+}(aq) + 4Cl^-(aq) \rightleftharpoons CuCl_4^{2-}(aq) + 4H_2O(l)$

or $Cu^{2+}(aq) + 4Cl^-(aq) \rightleftharpoons CuCl_4^{2-}(aq)$

(b) Since K_{st} for $CuCl_4^{2-}$ is so much smaller than for $Cu(NH_3)_4^{2+}$, the concentration of free Cu^{2+} ions in the solution of $CuCl_4^{2-}$ is far greater than can remain in contact with any but the smallest concentration of NH_3. The first equilibrium shifts to the right, removing free Cu^{2+} ions from the second equilibrium, which therefore shifts to the left until virtually no $CuCl_4^{2-}$ ions remain in solution.

Exercise 35

(a) The orange colour of $Fe^{3+}(aq)$ changes to purple when the 2-hydroxybenzoic acid is added, due to the formation of a small amount of a complex ion (represented as $Fe(hb)_2^+$). As edta is added, it removes Fe^{3+} from the solution by forming the very stable complex $Fe(edta)^-$. When virtually all the free Fe^{3+} has combined, the equilibrium

$$Fe^{3+}(aq) + 2hb^-(aq) \rightleftharpoons Fe(hb)_2^+(aq)$$

shifts so far to the left that the violet colour disappears, leaving the yellow colour of the $Fe(edta)^-$ ion.

(b) $Fe^{3+}(aq) + edta^{4-}(aq) \rightleftharpoons Fe(edta)^-(aq)$

Since edta solutions are usually made from the disodium salt, the following equation is probably better.

$$Fe^{3+}(aq) + H_2(edta)^{2-}(aq) \rightleftharpoons Fe(edta)^-(aq) + 2H^+(aq)$$

(c) Because K_{st} is so large, we can deduce from the equation that at the end-point:

amount of edta added = amount of Fe^{3+} in original solution

$\therefore\ 0.020\ dm^3 \times 0.10\ mol\ dm^3 = 0.025\ dm^3 \times x\ mol\ dm^{-3}$

$\therefore\ x = \dfrac{0.020 \times 0.10}{0.025} = 0.080$

i.e. $[Fe^{3+}(aq)] = \boxed{0.080\ mol\ dm^{-3}}$

Exercise 36

C.N. = 2. Linear, e.g. $Ag(NH_3)_2^+$ $H_3N{-}Ag{-}NH_3$

C.N. = 4. Tetrahedral, e.g. $Zn(NH_3)_4^{2+}$; or square planar, e.g. $CuCl_4^{2-}$

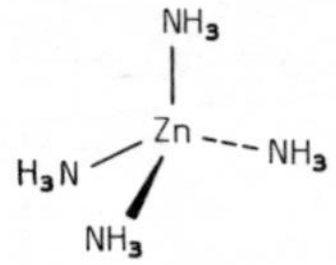

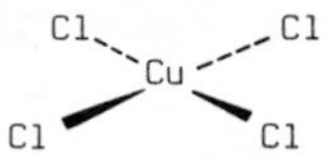

C.N. = 6. Octahedral, e.g. $Fe(CN)_6^{3-}$

(Note that this shape is symmetrical - all six points are equivalent, and three equivalent square planes can be identified as shown below.)

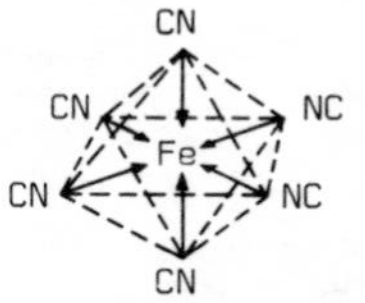

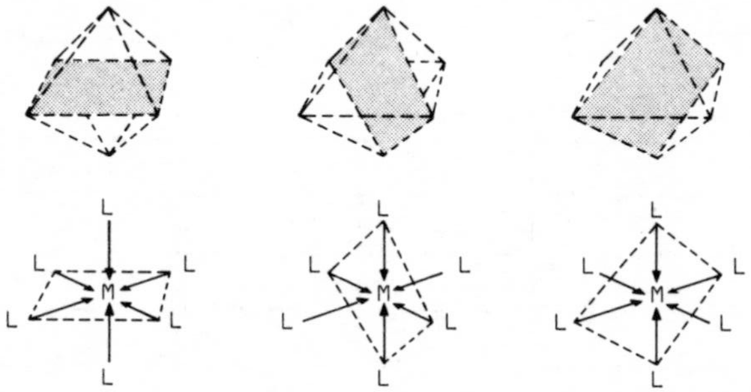

Exercise 37

(a) $Cr(H_2O)_5Cl^+$ and $Cr(H_2O)_5Br^+$ (with Br^- and Cl^- respectively).

(b) The ions are octahedral.

(c) Structural isomerism - the atoms are bonded differently. (Some texts call this ionization isomerism - a subdivision of structural isomerism. We do not consider subdivision to be necessary at this level.)

Exercise 38

(a) Since A does not lose water over concentrated sulphuric acid, the water molecules are more firmly bonded than mere water of crystallization - they must be ligands. Also, the precipitation of 3 mol of silver chloride from 1 mol of A shows that the chlorine is in the form of separate ions (3 per 'molecule' of A) rather than ligands. The fourth ion must be $Cr(H_2O)_6^{3+}$. 6-coordinated complexes are always octahedral; thus A must be:

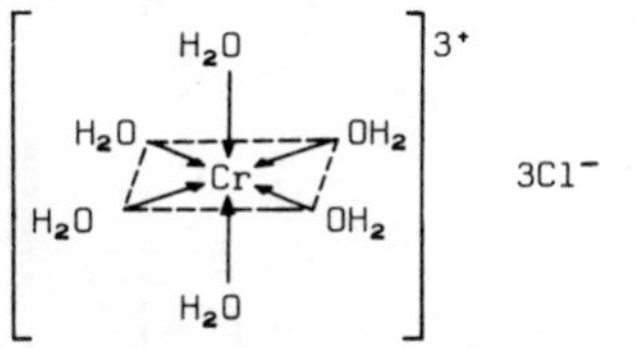

Since 1 mol of B loses 2 mol of water fairly readily, only 4 mol can be bonded as ligands, the other 2 mol being water of crystallization attached by weak van der Waals bonds. The immediate precipitation of 1 mol of silver chloride from 1 mol of B shows that only one chloride ion is 'free' and the other two are ligands. B must therefore be either:

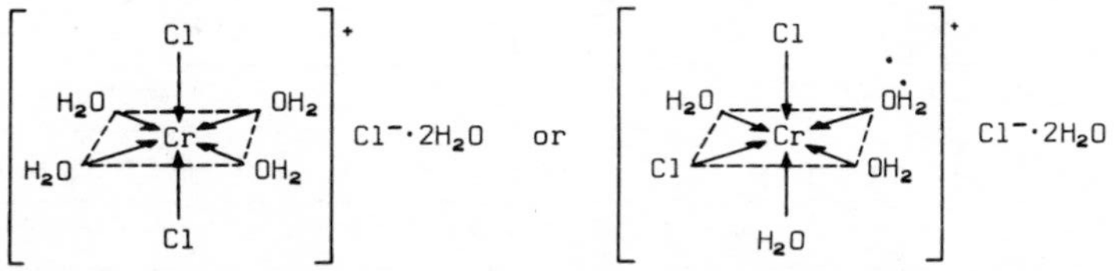

The additional 2 mol of silver chloride are precipitated slowly as chloride ligands are replaced by water molecules so that the structure, and colour, of the complex reverts to A.

Similar reasoning shows that C must be:

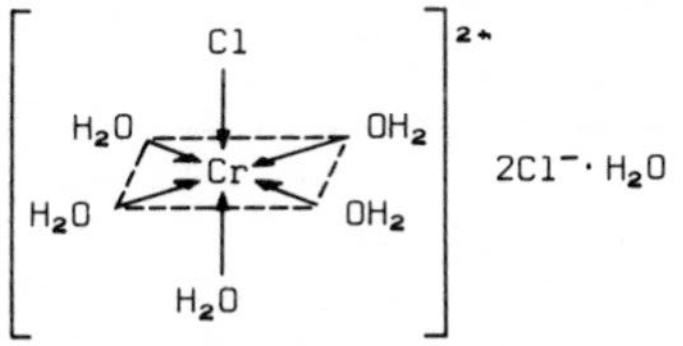

(b) A fourth compound with the same formula could be:

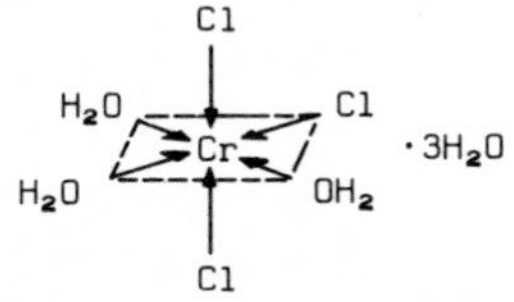

In this structure the 3+ charge on the central chromium ion is cancelled by the negative charges on three chloride ligands so that overall there would be no charge. A solution of this compound would not conduct electricity or react with silver nitrate until chloride ligands become replaced by water molecules.

Exercise 39

(a) Compound B would conduct electricity readily in aqueous solution because it is ionic. Compound A would not conduct readily in aqueous solution.

(b) The two species in solution would almost certainly have different colours. If there is an equilibrium we should be able to observe a shift in equilibrium position as a colour change. The equilibrium could be shifted in one direction by adding sodium chloride to increase $[Cl^-]$ and in the other by adding, say, $Ag^+(aq)$ to lower $[Cl^-]$.

Exercise 40

There are two isomeric ions, as shown below.

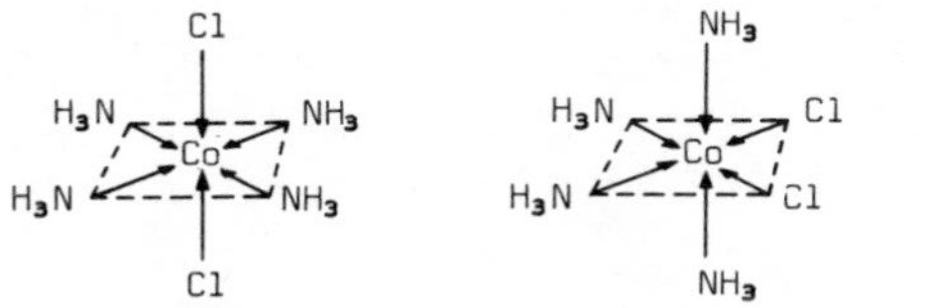

trans *cis*

(If you have drawn more than two, look closely at your sketches and you will see that the two Cl^- ligands are either opposite (*trans*) or adjacent (*cis*). Remember that all six points of a regular octahedron are equivalent - see our answer to Exercise 36.)

Exercise 41

(a) $Cr(NH_3)_4en^{3+}$ is not optically active. The plane represented by the shaded square is a plane of symmetry - it divides the ion into two identical and superimposable halves. Mirror images of the complete ion, e.g. as shown below, are identical and superimposable.

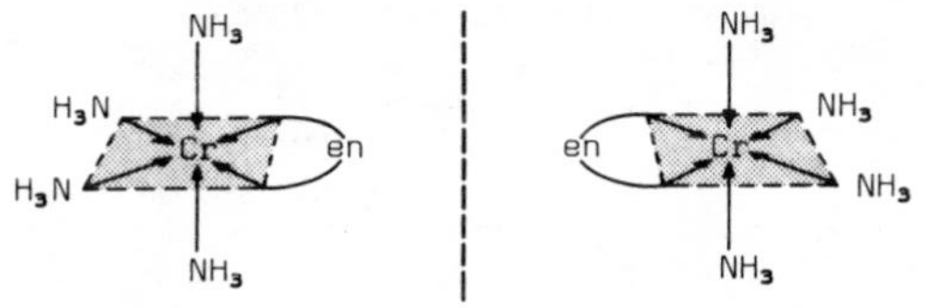

mirror

(b) There are two geometric isomers of $Cr(NH_3)_2(en)_2^{3+}$:

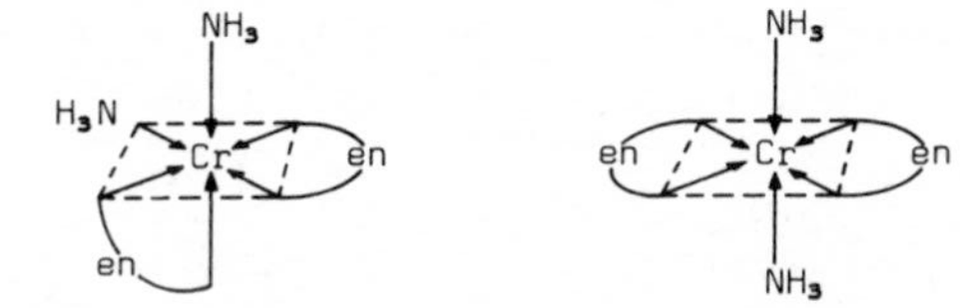

cis *trans*

The *cis*-isomer is optically active - there is no plane of symmetry, and mirror images cannot be superimposed. (Diagrams overleaf.)

Exercise 41 (cont.)

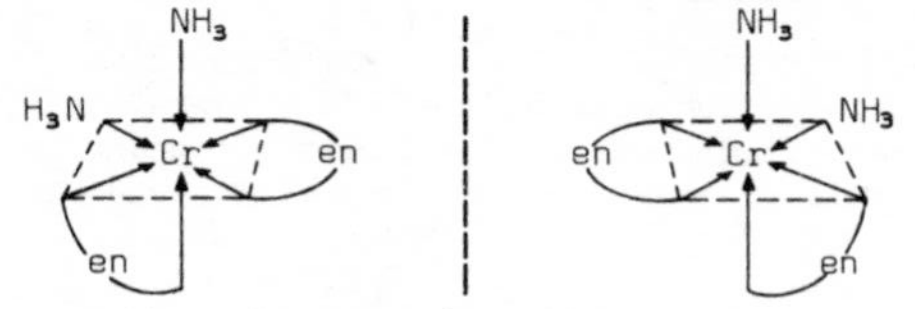

Thus, there are three isomers altogether.

(c) There are two optical isomers of $Cr(en)_3^{3+}$:

Experiment 4. Specimen results

Results Table 4

Tube number	1	2	3	4	5	6	7	8
Volume of $(NH_4)_2SO_4/cm^3$	15	5	5	5	5	5	5	5
Volume of $CuSO_4/cm^3$	0	1.0	1.5	2.0	2.5	3.0	4.0	5.0
Volume of NH_3/cm^3	0	9.0	8.5	8.0	7.5	7.0	6.0	5.0
Colorimeter reading	0	0.20	0.29	0.34	0.32	0.28	0.22	0.15

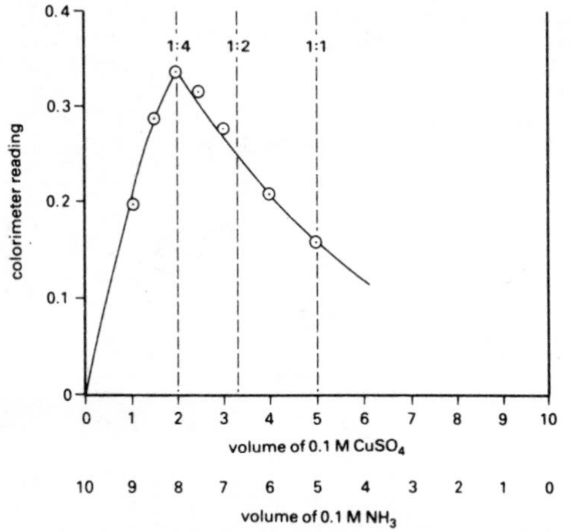

The maximum absorbance for a ratio $CuSO_4$: NH_3 = 1 : 4 indicates that the formula is $Cu(NH_3)_4^{2+}$.

Experiment 4. Questions

1. The addition of ammonia solution to copper sulphate solution usually causes precipitation of pale blue copper hydroxide:

$$NH_3(aq) + H_2O(l) \rightleftharpoons NH_4^+(aq) + OH^-(aq)$$

or

$$Cu^{2+}(aq) + 2OH^-(aq) \rightarrow Cu(OH)_2(s)$$

However, the addition of ammonium sulphate reduces $[OH^-(aq)]$ so much, by the common ion effect, that precipitation does not occur.

2. Although the amount of copper present increases, there is less and less ammonia present to convert it into the highly-coloured complex ion. The concentration of the complex ion and, therefore, the absorbance, decreases.

3. Although the amount of ammonia decreases, there is always an excess up to the peak, so that the concentration of complex ion increases as the amount of copper present increases.

4. In the unlikely event of your choosing a filter which was selective enough to pass only light which could be absorbed by $Cu(H_2O)_4^{2+}$ and not by $Cu(NH_3)_4^{2+}$, absorbance readings would increase throughout the experiment. In practice, however, both filtering and absorbing occur over a band of wavelengths, and a certain amount of absorbance will occur using any filter. Using the wrong filter in this experiment would still give the same final result although the peak would be less pronounced. More care may be necessary in other experiments where species of different colours with similar intensities may be present.

5. Since the colour of $Cu(NH_3)_4^{2+}(aq)$ is far more intense than that of $Cu(H_2O)_4^{2+}(aq)$, reasonable results can be obtained in this experiment by using no filter at all! You were asked to use a filter to establish the general principle, which may be far more important in other similar experiments.

Exercise 42

One might expect the formation of $V(H_2O)_6^{4+}$ ions in solution initially. However, V^{4+}, having a high charge, would greatly polarize the surrounding water molecules. This would cause the release of H^+ ions to make the solution strongly acidic (as in the Worked Example).

$$V(H_2O)_6^{4+}(aq) + H_2O(l) \rightarrow V(H_2O)_5OH^{3+}(aq) + H_3O^+(aq)$$

In this case, further reaction is favoured because the resulting ion is still highly charged, so that another H^+ ion is released.

$$V(H_3O)_5OH^{3+}(aq) + H_2O(l) \rightarrow V(H_2O)_4O^{2+}(aq) + H_3O^+$$

The four coordinated water molecules are frequently omitted from the formula, so that the ion is often represented as $VO^{2+}(aq)$.

(Note that it is not clear why both protons are removed from the same water molecule, rather than from adjacent molecules to give $V(OH)_2(H_2O)_4^{2+}$. Species like this, such as $Fe(OH)_2(H_2O)_4^+$, are known to exist.)

Exercise 43

(a) Mn^{7+} would have such a high polarizing power that all the protons from four attached water molecules would be released:

$$Mn(H_2O)_4^{7+}(aq) \rightarrow MnO_4^-(aq) + 8H^+(aq)$$

(b) The term complex ion is usually reserved for species where the ligands can be fairly easily removed, and both ligand and cation can have an independent existence in solution. In this case, neither $Mn^{7+}(aq)$ nor $O^{2-}(aq)$ can be identified in solution. (O^{2-} in soluble solids reacts with water to form $OH^-(aq)$.)

Exercise 44

(a) $MnO_4^-(aq) + 8H^+(aq) + 5e^- \rightleftharpoons Mn^{2+}(aq) + 4H_2O(l)$

(b) $E^{\ominus}$ = 1.51 V refers to standard conditions where $[H^+(aq)]$ = 1.0 mol dm^{-3}, i.e. pH = 0. If the pH is increased to 1, $[H^+(aq)]$ is decreased and the equilibrium shifts to the left so that $E^{\ominus}$ becomes less positive.

The Nernst equation can be applied:

$$E = E^{\ominus} + \frac{RT}{ZF} \times ln \left(\frac{\text{concentrations of oxidized forms raised to powers}}{\text{concentrations of reduced forms raised to powers}}\right)$$

In this case, the new value of E is given by:

$$E = 1.51\text{ V} + \frac{8.31\text{ J K}^{-1}\text{ mol}^{-1} \times 298\text{ K}}{5 \times 9.65 \times 10^4\text{ J V}^{-1}} \times ln\left(\frac{[MnO_4^-(aq)][H^+(aq)]^8}{[Mn^{2+}(aq)]}\right)$$

$$= 1.51\text{ V} + (5.13 \times 10^{-3}\text{ V} \times ln\left(\frac{1.00 \times (0.100)^8}{1.00}\right) \quad \text{(omitting units)}$$

$$= 1.51\text{ V} + (5.13 \times 10^{-3}\text{ V} \times -18.4) = 1.51\text{ V} - 0.094\text{ V} = \boxed{1.42\text{ V}}$$

Exercise 45

(a) (i) No reaction, because $\Delta E^{\ominus}$ is negative for:

$$2Fe^{2+}(aq) + I_2(aq) \rightleftharpoons 2Fe^{3+}(aq) + 2I^-(aq);$$
$$\Delta E^{\ominus} = 0.54\text{ V} - 0.77\text{ V} = -0.23\text{ V}$$

(ii) The brown colour of iodine would be discharged because a redox reaction occurs ($\Delta E^{\ominus}$ positive):

$$2Fe(CN)_6^{4-}(aq) + I_2(aq) \rightleftharpoons 2Fe(CN)_6^{3-}(aq) + 2I^-(aq);$$
$$\Delta E^{\ominus} = 0.54\text{ V} - 0.36\text{ V} = +0.18\text{ V}$$

(b) (i) A brown coloration of iodine would appear because a redox reaction occurs ($\Delta E^{\ominus}$ positive):

$$2Fe^{3+}(aq) + 2I^-(aq) \rightleftharpoons 2Fe^{2+}(aq) + I_2(aq);\ \Delta E^{\ominus} = +0.23\text{ V}$$

(This is the reverse of the equation in (a) (i).)

(ii) No change, because $\Delta E^{\ominus}$ is negative for:

$$2Fe(CN)_6^{3-}(aq) + 2I^-(aq) \rightleftharpoons 2Fe(CN)_6^{4-}(aq) + I_2(aq);\ \Delta E^{\ominus} = -0.18\text{ V}$$

(This is the reverse of the equation in (a) (ii).)

(c) It is easier to oxidize iron(II) to iron(III), and harder to reduce iron(III) to iron(II), when cyanide ions rather than water molecules are ligands.

Exercise 46

(a) Although dioxophosphoric acid should be able to reduce Cu(II) to Cu(I) ($\Delta E^{\ominus}$ = 0.15 V - (-0.50 V) = 0.65 V) it would probably reduce Cu(I) to Cu(0) even more readily ($\Delta E^{\ominus}$ = 0.52 V - (-0.50 V) = 1.02 V). The net result therefore would be reduction to copper metal.

(b) Copper(II) ions and copper metal would be produced if copper(I) sulphate were dissolved in water. The second and third half-cells combine to give a cell in which the reaction occurs:

$$Cu^+(aq) + Cu^+(aq) \rightleftharpoons Cu(s) + Cu^{2+}(aq);\ \Delta E^{\ominus} = 0.52\text{ V} - 0.15\text{ V} = 0.37\text{ V}$$

This type of change, simultaneous oxidation and reduction of the same species, is called disproportionation.

Exercise 47

(a) The attempt would probably be successful, because the reduction of copper(II) to copper(I) is favoured ($\Delta E^{\ominus}$ positive):

$$2Cu^{2+}(aq) + 8CN^-(aq) + H_3PO_2(aq) + H_2O(l) \rightleftharpoons 2Cu(CN)_4^{3-}(aq)$$
$$+ H_3PO_3(aq) + 2H^+(aq);\ \Delta E^{\ominus} = 1.77\text{ V} - (-0.50\text{ V}) = +2.27\text{ V}$$

whereas the further reduction of copper(I) to copper(0) is not favoured ($\Delta E^{\ominus}$ negative):

$$2Cu(CN)_4^{3-}(aq) + H_3PO_2(aq) + H_2O(l) \rightleftharpoons 2Cu(s) + 8CN^-(aq) + H_3PO_3(aq)$$
$$+ 2H^+(aq);\ \Delta E^{\ominus} = -1.09\text{ V} - (-0.50\text{ V}) = -0.59\text{ V}$$

(b) Copper would probably be an effective reducing agent:

$$Cu(s) + Cu^{2+}(aq) + 4CN^-(aq) \rightleftharpoons Cu^+(aq) + Cu(CN)_4^{3-}(aq);$$
$$\Delta E^{\ominus} = 1.77\text{ V} - 0.52\text{ V} = +1.25\text{ V}$$

With an excess of cyanide ions, the following reaction occurs:

$$Cu^+(aq) + 4CN^-(aq) \rightleftharpoons Cu(CN)_4^{3-}(aq)$$

The overall reaction is therefore:

$$Cu(s) + Cu^{2+}(aq) + 8CN^-(aq) \rightleftharpoons 2Cu(CN)_4^{3-}(aq)$$

Experiment 5. Questions - parts A and B

1. The white solid is copper(I) chloride, CuCl. Colour in the transition elements is associated with partly-filled *d*-orbitals. Cu(I) has a partly filled set of *d*-orbitals - $1s^2 2s^2 2p^6 3s^2 3p^6 3d^{10}$.
2. In part A, the reducing agent is copper(0), in part B it is sulphur(IV).
3. Heat was required in part A because the reaction involved a solid - such reactions are often slow at room temperature.
4. The excess of chloride ions stabilizes the Cu(I) oxidation state in a complex ion so that reduction of Cu(II) to Cu(I) can proceed in solution.
5. The dark brown colour is due to the increasing concentration of the copper(I) complex $CuCl_4^{3-}$ as it is formed from the green/yellow $CuCl_4^{2-}$.
6. $Cu^+(aq)$, present in very small concentration, is oxidized by air to $Cu^{2+}(aq)$. The equilibrium

$$CuCl(s) \rightleftharpoons Cu^+(aq) + Cl^-(aq)$$

is then shifted to the right to allow further oxidation of $Cu^+(aq)$ to $Cu^{2+}(aq)$, eventually giving a blue solution.

Experiment 5. Questions - part C

1. A muddy brownish suspension is formed. On settling, the precipitate appears creamy-coloured and the solution brown.
2. The thiosulphate removes the brown coloration, leaving a clear solution over a creamy precipitate. The brown coloration must therefore have been due to iodine.
3. Since iodide has been oxidized to iodine, copper(II) must have been reduced to copper(I).
4. The creamy-white precipitate must therefore be copper(I) iodide, CuI.

Results Table 5

	Method	Observations	Equation(s)
A. Preparation of copper(I) chloride.	Heat copper(II) chloride, copper and excess sodium chloride in a little water. Dilute.	The green solution darkened slowly to almost black. A white ppt. appeared on dilution.	$CuCl_2(aq) + Cu(s) \rightarrow 2CuCl(s)$ (via $CuCl_4^{2-}$ and $CuCl_4^{3-}$)
B. Preparation of copper(I) chloride.	Mix solutions of copper(II) chloride and sulphite ions.	A white precipitate appeared.	$2CuCl_2(aq) + SO_3^{2-}(aq) + H_2O(l) \rightarrow 2CuCl(s) + SO_4^{2-}(aq) + 2HCl(aq)$
C. Preparation of copper(I) iodide.	Mix solutions of copper(II) sulphate and potassium iodide. Add sodium thiosulphate.	A muddy brown suspension was formed. Adding thiosulphate left a cream ppt. and a clear solution.	$2Cu^{2+}(aq) + 4I^-(aq) \rightarrow 2CuI(s) + I_2(aq)$ $I_2(aq) + 2S_2O_3^{2-}(aq) \rightarrow 2I^-(aq) + S_4O_6^{2-}(aq)$

Exercise 48

(a) Iodide ions would not be expected to reduce copper(II) to copper(I) because $\Delta E^\ominus$ is negative for the reaction:

$$2Cu^{2+}(aq) + 2I^-(aq) \rightleftharpoons 2Cu^+(aq) + I_2(aq)$$

(b) For $Cu^+(aq) + I^-(aq) \rightleftharpoons CuI(s)$ $\quad \Delta E^\ominus = 0.15\text{ V} - 0.54\text{ V} = -0.39\text{ V}$

$$K_c = \frac{1}{[Cu^+(aq)][I^-(aq)]} = 1.0 \times 10^{12}\text{ mol}^{-2}\text{ dm}^6$$

$$\therefore \quad [Cu^+(aq)] = \frac{1}{1.0 \times 10^{12}\text{ mol}^{-2}\text{ dm}^6} \times 0.10\text{ mol dm}^{-3}$$

$$= 1.0 \times 10^{-11}\text{ mol dm}^{-3}$$

(c) If $[Cu^+(aq)]$ is made very small, the half-cell equilibrium

$$Cu^{2+}(aq) + e^- \rightleftharpoons Cu^+(aq)$$

is shifted to the right and $E^\ominus$ is made more positive.

The Nernst equation can be applied:

$$E = E^\ominus + \frac{RT}{ZF}\log_e\frac{[\text{oxidized form}]}{[\text{reduced form}]}$$

$$= 0.15\text{ V} + \frac{8.31\text{ J K}^{-1}\text{ mol}^{-1} \times 298\text{ K}}{1 \times 9.65 \times 10^4\text{ J V}^{-1}} \times 2.30\log_{10}\frac{1.0\text{ mol dm}^{-3}}{1.0 \times 10^{-11}\text{ mol dm}^{-3}}$$

$$= 0.15\text{ V} + 0.65\text{ V} = \boxed{0.80\text{ V}}$$

Exercise 48 (cont.)

(d) Despite the fact that $\Delta E^\ominus$ is negative for the reduction of copper(II) to copper(I) by iodide, the reaction proceeds to an equilibrium position where $[Cu^+(aq)]$, though very small, is high enough to cause precipitation of copper(I) iodide.

Because the electrode potential for bromine is so much higher than for iodine, the equilibrium position for the reduction of copper(II) to copper(I) by bromide ion lies even further to the left:

$$2Cu^{2+}(aq) + 2Br^-(aq) \rightleftharpoons 2Cu^+(aq) + Br_2(aq);$$

$$\Delta E^\ominus = 0.54\text{ V} - 1.09\text{ V} = -0.55\text{ V}$$

Consequently, $[Cu^+(aq)]$ is not high enough to precipitate copper(I) bromide.

Experiment 6. Questions

1. Carbon dioxide from the redox reaction, and oxygen from the decomposition of hydrogen peroxide, which is also catalysed by Co^{2+}.
2. The dark green colour is due to a complex ion of Co(III) with 2,3-dihydroxybutanedioate ions as ligands. The green colour disappears as this complex completes the oxidation of excess 2,3-dihydroxybutanedioate and is itself reduced back to Co(II).
3. The green colour persists for some time at room temperature because the reaction between the Co(III) complex and 2,3-dihydroxybutanedioate ion is slow.

Experiment 7. Specimen results

Results Table 6

Transition element		Chromium	Manganese	Iron
Oxidation states used		Cr(VI) Cr(III)	Mn(VII) Mn(II)	Fe(III) Fe(II)
Electrode potential/V (higher ox. state ⇌ lower)		1.33	1.51	0.77
Electrode potential/V ($I_2 + 2e^- \rightleftharpoons 2I^-$)		0.54	0.54	0.54
Electrode potential/V ($S_2O_8^{2-} + 2e^- \rightleftharpoons 2SO_4^{2-}$)		2.01	2.01	2.01
Does higher ox. state oxidize I^-?	Prediction	Yes	Yes	Yes
	Practically	Yes	Yes	Yes
Does lower state reduce $S_2O_8^{2-}$?	Prediction	Yes	Yes	Yes
	Practically	No	No	No
Do you expect catalysis?		No	No	Yes
Time for blue colour to appear/s		Varies with conditions		

Experiment 7. Questions

1. Iron is an effective catalyst, both as Fe(II) and Fe(III). A simplified mechanism might consist of two steps, either of which could come first:

   Fe(II) reacts with peroxodisulphate → Fe(III) and sulphate.

   Fe(III) reacts with iodide → Fe(II) and iodine.

2. Chromium cannot function as a catalyst because Cr(III) will not react with peroxodisulphate. This is clearly a kinetic effect, because $\Delta E^\ominus$ is favourable.

3. Manganese(VII) functions well as a catalyst even though Mn(II) will not react with peroxodisulphate. Another oxidation state - Mn(III), Mn(IV) or Mn(VI) - could be produced as an intermediate.

4. Laboratory temperatures can vary considerably over two days (or even over a double period, or in different parts of the room!). As you have learned, temperature changes have a marked effect on rates of reaction and could make it difficult to decide whether a particular species has and could make it difficult to decide whether catalysis has occurred.

Exercise 49

(a) A single line shows how the standard free energy change for a given reaction varies with temperature. The reaction is usually the combination of an element with one mole of oxygen.

(b) Using $\Delta G^\ominus = \Delta H^\ominus - T\Delta S^\ominus$ and assuming $\Delta H^\ominus$ and $\Delta S^\ominus$ are constant:

	$2C(s) + O_2(g) \rightarrow 2CO(g)$		$2Fe(s) + O_2(g) \rightarrow 2FeO(s)$	
Temperature/K	$T\Delta S^\ominus$/kJ mol^{-1}	$\Delta G^\ominus$/kJ mol^{-1}	$T\Delta S^\ominus$/kJ mol^{-1}	$\Delta G^\ominus$/kJ mol^{-1}
(i) 298	298 x 0.180 = 53.6	-221 - 53.6 = -275	298 x (-0.151) = -45.0	-533 (-45.0) = -488
(ii) 1000	1000 x 0.180 = 180	-221 - 180 = -401	1000 x (-0.151) = -151	-533 - (-151) = -382
(iii) 1500	1500 x 0.180 = 270	-221 - 270 = -491	1500 x (-0.151) = -227	-533 - (-227) = -306
(iv) 1693	1693 x 0.180 = 305	-221 - 305 = -526	1693 x (-0.151) = -256	-533 - (-256) = -277
(v) 1808	1808 x 0.180 = 325	-221 - 325 = -546	1808 x (-0.151) = -273	-533 - (-273) = -260
(vi) 2000	2000 x 0.180 = 360	-221 - 360 = -581	2000 x (-0.151) = -302	-533 - (-302) = -231

(c)

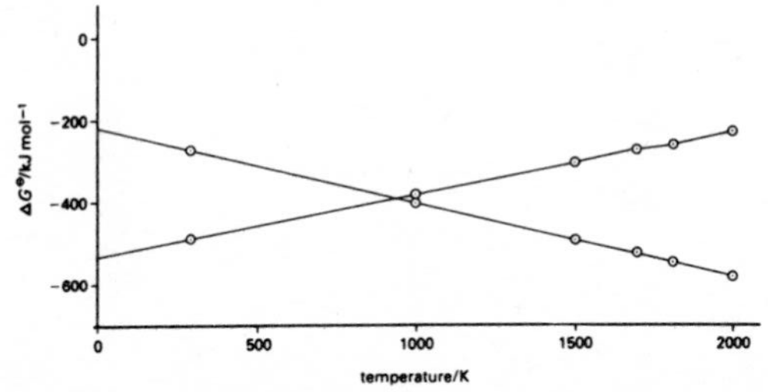

Exercise 49 (cont.)

(d) 1693 K and 1808 K are the melting-points of FeO and Fe respectively. There are discontinuities at these temperatures because of the free energy changes associated with a change of state.

(Note that these discontinuities are not always shown in simple diagrams since they are usually of secondary importance.)

(e) The C → CO line has a negative slope because $\Delta S^\ominus$ is positive for a reaction which increases the number of gas molecules. Consequently, $\Delta G^\ominus$ decreases with increasing temperature.

The Fe → FeO line has a positive slope because $\Delta S^\ominus$ is negative for a reaction which decreases the number of gas molecules. Consequently, $\Delta G^\ominus$ increases with increasing temperature.

Exercise 50

(a) Iron(II) oxide might be reduced by carbon at temperatures above 700 °C.

The equation for the reaction is obtained by subtracting the equations:

$2C(s) + O_2(g) \rightarrow 2CO(g);\quad \Delta G_1^\ominus$
$2Fe(s) + O_2(g) \rightarrow 2FeO(s);\quad \Delta G_2^\ominus$
$2C(s) + 2FeO(s) \rightarrow 2Fe(s) + 2CO(g);\quad \Delta G_3^\ominus = \Delta G_1^\ominus - \Delta G_2^\ominus$

At all temperatures above 700 °C, $\Delta G_1^\ominus < \Delta G_2^\ominus$, so that $\Delta G_3^\ominus$ is negative and the reaction is feasible.

Below 700 °C, $\Delta G_1^\ominus > \Delta G_2^\ominus$, so that $\Delta G_3^\ominus$ is positive and the reaction is not feasible.

(b) Iron(II) oxide might be reduced by carbon monoxide at temperatures below 700 °C.

The equation for the reaction is obtained by subtracting the two equations below.

$2CO(g) + O_2(g) \rightarrow 2CO_2(g);\quad \Delta G_4^\ominus$
$2Fe(s) + O_2(g) \rightarrow 2FeO(s);\quad \Delta G_1^\ominus$
$2CO(g) + 2FeO(s) \rightarrow 2Fe(s) + 2CO_2(g);\quad \Delta G_5^\ominus = \Delta G_4^\ominus - \Delta G_1^\ominus$

At all temperatures above 700 °C, $\Delta G_4^\ominus > \Delta G_1^\ominus$, so that $\Delta G_5^\ominus$ is positive and the reaction is not feasible.

Below 700 °C, $\Delta G_4^\ominus < \Delta G_1^\ominus$, so that $\Delta G_5^\ominus$ is negative and the reaction is feasible. (Note, however, that despite the favourable energetics at low temperatures, the reaction becomes slower and slower as the temperature falls.)

Exercise 51

(a) Incorrect. $\Delta G^\ominus$ is positive below 1200 °C.

(b) Correct. $\Delta G^\ominus$ is negative at all temperatures shown on the diagram.

(c) Incorrect. $\Delta G^\ominus$ is positive below 450 °C.

(d) Correct. $\Delta G^\ominus$ is negative above 350 °C for reduction by carbon and above 300 °C for reduction by hydrogen.